W9-AAF-782

Michael Foss

# chívalry

David McKay Company, Inc.
New York

CHIVALRY

Copyright © 1975 by Michael Foss

All rights reserved, including the right to reproduce
this book, or parts thereof, in any form, except for
the inclusion of brief quotations in a review.

Published in Great Britain by Book Club Associates
First American Edition, 1976

Designed by Harold Bartram
Picture research by Celestine Dars
Production Director John Ford

ISBN 0-679-50681-0
Library of Congress Catalog Card Number: 76-15900

Printed in Great Britain

# contents

21.668

# chapter one

Aggrieved and incredulous, like one who sees nature overturned, the historian Ammianus Marcellinus recorded an unthinkable event: on the fifth day of the Ides of August in A.D. 378 the imperial Roman infantry, the world-conquerors of antiquity, were annihilated by a rabble of Teutonic cavalry.

At Adrianople, under a vertical sun, the army of the Emperor Valens prepared for a weary, familiar task, defending the lands of the civilized against barbarian attack. Advancing eight miles over the parched Greek hillside the Roman army came to a circle of waggons behind which the German tribes awaited, large men with wild looks, some in skins and some in shirt-mail, some swinging clubs and pikes, and others the dreaded *spatha*, the long sword that scythed so easily through buckler, mail and limbs. Derisive and hideous yells sustained the courage of the Germans against the steady ranks of infantry. A premature charge by the Roman auxiliaries dissolved against the rampart of the waggons. The heat-scarred veterans, suffering under the noon sun and weak from thirst and hunger, were dismayed. At this moment the large body of German cavalry swept out of the mountains like a thunderbolt and crashed upon the legions. The Roman cavalry, covering the foot-soldiers, fled. The unsupported infantry held, but were driven so close together by the furious charge that they had no room to wield their weapons and hardly room to draw them. Billowing dust covered the field like poisonous gas through which penetrated the hiss of weapons, the animal shouts of the victorious and the no less animal cries of the dying. Feet slipped on a slime of blood and dust. The high sun pierced exhausted bodies staggering amid the cruel patterns of the barbarian cavalry. 'One black pool of blood disfigured all,' wrote the aghast historian, 'and wherever the eye turned, it could see nothing but piles of dead, and

The early barbarian horseman, descendant of the steppe nomad, riding, apparently, without saddle or stirrup. Ornamental shield plaque of the Lombard period, *c.* A.D. 600, from San Pietro Stabio, Switzerland.

Pagan warriors of the barbaric and formidable Germanic tribes, bearing typical arms of sword, spear and axe. Bronze matrices from a helmet of the Vandal period, *c*. 7th Cent, from Torslunda in Sweden.

corpses trampled on without mercy.' Implacable horsemen, drunk on blood and victory, buried the groans of despair under more terrible shouts of triumph, and spurred their horses after fleeing Romans. The Emperor Valens, the generals of foot and horse, the Count of the Palace, thirty-five commanders and forty thousand men of the legions fell before a moonless night hid the devastated field.

Hooves of Teutonic cavalry broke up the fabric of the Roman Empire. Armed horsemen dragged covers of anarchy across old civilization, covers pieced out with crimson patches of blood-letting. Horse and rider, bred in tumultuous savagery on the wide lands beyond the Caspian, savoured the bitter taste of plunder and destruction. Born to the saddle, despising mere foot-soldiers, they showed a variety of stratagems, to the confusion of infantry and the decay of society. The scalding rain of arrows shot at the gallop by Herules, Gepids, and Huns silenced the old military prejudices of the Empire. The new horse-archers were men to fear, protected by cuirass and greaves, armed with bow and sword and sometimes a lance, with a small shield handily slung from the left shoulder. 'They are excellent riders,' wrote one who saw them in action, 'can shoot while galloping at full speed, and keep up a flight of arrows with equal ease advancing or retreating. They draw the bow-string not to the breast but to the face, or even to the right ear, so that the arrow always flies strongly enough to inflict a deadly wound, easily piercing both shield and cuirass.' More fearsome still was the heavy cavalry of Goth and Lombard, with crested helm and enveloping coat of mail, bearing shield and mace and axe and long sword, but most terribly, wielding the great lance by which Paul the Deacon recorded a Byzantine horseman transfixed, jerked from the saddle and carried along twitching like an insect on a pin.

They raged at will across Roman lands, cruel, courageous warriors, distrusting roads and houses, some professedly Christian, though tainted with strange heresies, many frankly pagan pulling on ox-carts the dark gods of distant forests. Bemused, perhaps intimidated, by inscriptions, aqueducts, marble pavements lined with cypress, contemptuous of men who avoided war and expended their energies in architecture, in the planting of groves and orchards, in the right ordering of words, they had only the primitive blood-loyalties of the war-band to keep them together amid the chaos caused by their swords and arrows and lances. 'They do no business public or private except in arms,' Tacitus had written of the German tribes. Strength and courage were their only virtues, loyalty to their war-chief their only honour, the banding together in the war-party almost their only organization. 'Real distinction and strength', Tacitus wrote, 'belong to the chief who has always around him a band of chosen warriors, to be a glory in peace and a protection in war.' Though peace had its rewards for men of reputation, only in war could a young man earn merit, proving himself ferocious amid any danger and so advancing into the favoured ranks of the chief's *comitatus*, the sole aristocracy of the tribe. Young men vied in recklessness and blood-lust under the approving eye of the chief. 'When the fighting begins,' wrote Tacitus, 'it is shameful for a chief to be outdone in bravery, and equally shameful for the followers not to match the courage of the leader: to survive one's chief and return from battle is a foul disgrace that lasts as long as life. To defend him, to support him, to turn one's own deeds to his glory, this is the main oath of their allegiance.' Peace was idleness and boredom, yawning in the sun, drinking from dawn to dawn, cracking heads in drunken brawls: 'it would be far harder to persuade them to plough the fields and wait for the year's yield than to challenge the enemy and earn a wage of wounds.' But the first sound of war gladdened the heart. Rising up from squalor and stupor, the tribal warrior took to his 'charger and murderous invincible spear', which were all he demanded from the liberality of the chief, welcoming the violence of war as the test of manhood, and the plunder of war as the reward of life.

A new age of blood and ignorance. Old, learned virtues perished, drowned by blood and ignorance. New virtue rested on the power of horse and lance. A singular figure rode ominously through the dark times, the select warrior of the chief's choosing, the man of the *comitatus*, whose superiority rested on horse and lance. Headlong, undisciplined courage made him a capricious death-dealing figure, bound to warfare but with no aim other than his own reputation and the glorification of the war-chief: he was the first knight.

Goths, Visigoths, Lombards, Franks—barbaric dynasties following one another over dark lands spurting sudden flames of conquest and destruction. The knights were ever at work. New waves of invaders, as relentless as winter seas, confirmed the importance of cavalry. The infantry of the Franks under Charles Martel had successfully stopped the advance of the Saracens, at Poitiers in 732: 'The men of the north', wrote the chronicler, 'stood as motionless

Charlemagne: silver statue from the sarcophagus in the Cathedral of Aachen, Charlemagne's capital city.

as a wall; they were like a belt of ice frozen together, and could not be dissolved, as they slew the Arabs with the sword.' But the continuance of the Frankish kingdom against so many enemies—Saracen in the south, Avar, Lombard, Bavarian in the east, Saxon and Frisian in the north—depended on the mobility and power of cavalry. Charlemagne saw to it that the Franks became horsemen and his capitularies ordained a large body of heavy cavalry. 'You shall come to the Weser', he wrote to his vassal, the Abbot of Altaich, in May 806, 'with your men prepared to go on warlike service to any part of our realm that we may point out: that is, you shall come with arms and gear and all warlike equipment of clothing and victuals. Every horseman shall have shield, lance, sword, dagger, a bow and a quiver. On your carts you shall have ready spades, axes, picks, and iron-pointed stakes, and all other things needed for the host. The rations shall be for three months, the clothing must last for six.' To neglect the least item was to risk the great King's anger.

Under such tutelage the cavalry of the Franks quickly learnt their business. Do not engage the Franks 'until you have secured all possible advantages for yourself', wrote the Byzantine Leo the Wise around 900, 'as their cavalry, with their long lances and large shields, charge with an overwhelming impetus'. This was the cavalry that secured the vast frontiers of Charlemagne's empire, from the

One of the oldest representations of the early knight, showing him well protected and heavily armed, wielding in particular the 'murderous, invincible' lance that opponents feared so much. An illustration from a 9th Cent psalter.

Carolingian knights on the march, some wearing the long surcoat of iron chain-mail and nearly all carrying the lance which was the chief weapon of heavy cavalry. An illustration from the 9th Cent Golden Psalter of St Gall.

Spanish Ebro to the German Elbe, from the North Sea to the Adriatic. These were the armed horsemen who beat back the most serious incursion of all, the Viking raids of the ninth and tenth centuries. The image of the successful Frankish soldier was the iron-clad knight—the image of Charlemagne himself descending on Pavia in 773, seen in the epic description of a monk of St Gall: 'Then appeared the iron king, crowned with his iron helm, with sleeves of iron-mail on his arms, his broad breast protected by an iron byrnie, an iron lance in his left hand, his right free to grasp his unconquered sword. His thighs were guarded with iron-mail, though other men are wont to leave them unprotected that they may spring the more lightly on their steeds. And his legs, like those of all his host, were protected by iron greaves. His shield was plain iron without device or colour. And round him and before and behind him rode all his men, armed as nearly like him as they could fashion themselves; so iron filled the fields and the ways, and the sun's rays were in every quarter reflected from iron, and the terrified citizens cried in their dismay, "Iron, iron everywhere!"'

Iron-clad knight, black figure of a blood-stained age. Tribal roots nourished power without responsibility; chaos in history bred brutality and wilfulness. The forces of the Frank, wrote Leo the Wise, the observer from civilized society, 'have no bonds of discipline, but only those of kindred or oath'. Possessing no idea of the State, hardly touched by morality or justice, superstitious rather than religious, the knights of the northern kingdoms were kept in hand only by an exceptional leader. Central authority, if it existed, was unimaginably distant; the king was just a warrior as you were, admired if strong, despised if weak. In the vast wastes of the land, in Carpathian solitudes, on Baltic salt-marshes, in the stony fastness of the Pyrenees, on the storm-coasts of the North Sea, who could tell friend from foe? A swirl of dust on the horizon announced unknown horsemen from the Asiatic plains; gaunt silhouettes appeared against a declining northern sun; the sudden echo of alien hooves filled a mountain pass; sails stood off a headland and then the dragon-beak of a lean ship nosed up an estuary: what threatening presences were these, looming over man and family, household and land?

How much was to be endured in the hope that some central authority, if it existed, under a king, who was only a warrior as you were, more or less strong, overcoming the limitations of his position, his poverty and ignorance, the vast weariness of his territories, could resolve your perplexities or bring you help in good time? On every side enemies gathered. Greek and Arab pirates patrolled the Mediterranean, a menace to all coastal settlements. The ancient port of Marseilles was a sure attraction, plundered in 848, threatened many times, and evidently regarded (together with its prosperous environs) as a fruitful source of victims for the Arab slave-markets. Saracen brigands, throughout the tenth century, commanded the Alpine passes and roamed abroad in the high country where they seemed, to the monks whose isolated monasteries they terrorized, as active as 'mountain goats'. The Monastery of Novalesa, above Susa, was sacked in 906. By the mid-century the robbers had penetrated to the far uplands of the Vaud and the Valais, where they burnt the Monastery of Saint-Maurice d'Agaune. Another band of Moslem raiders had the temerity to besiege the famous house of St Gall, and shot the monks as they walked in procession about the church. Otto the Great, attempting to emulate Charlemagne, none the less failed in the Christian mission of clearing these infidels from the land. The task was not done until William of Provence, outraged by the capture and ransom of his friend and confessor the Abbot of Cluny, took revenge on the main Saracen fortress at Le Freinet in 975.

Further to the east, on the edge of the European lands, there arose out of the everlasting dust of the steppes, with the characteristic suddenness of nomads, the Hungarian, or Magyar, tribes. Pressed from behind by puzzling migrations of other Asiatic hordes, the Hungarians packed their felt tents, drove herds and horses to the west. Crossing the Carpathians soon after 860 they were laying waste Bavaria and the Valley of the Po by 900. Six years later they were over the Elbe and into Saxony. The year 917 saw them sheltered in the forests of the Vosges; by 924 their headlong gallop had taken them as far as Otranto, in southern Italy, and Nîmes in France where, the chronicler joyfully reported, they went down to a 'plague of dysentery'. From the grazing grounds of the Danube they made

An antler carved in the form of a Viking head, 11th Cent, from Sigtuna in Sweden.

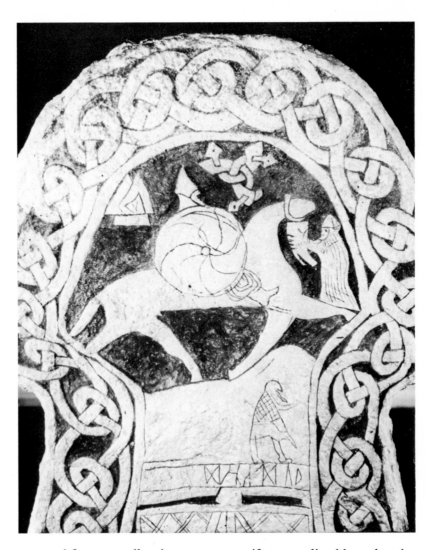

Mounted Viking warrior, showing that the Northmen were familiar with cavalry as early as the 8th Cent. Stone carving from Lillbjars in Gotland, *c.* 8th Cent.

seasonal forays to all points west, as swift, unpredictable and malevolent as a parched east wind. Extortion and plunder was their business, destroying what they could not take away on horse or cart. Walled towns were safe from them, for they had neither the means nor the patience for a siege. But all outlying districts were at risk. Populations were put to the sword, excepting only the women and young boys whom the nomads kept for their own nameless pleasures, and for the future profit of Greek slave-dealers: a noble girl of Worms was captured in 954 and offered for sale in the market of her own city. A century of damage was to pass before these rootless predators began to feel the suave invitations of civilization, settled, crowned a king and became a nation.

Saracen and Magyar, in the south and east, contrived much pain for the settled peoples of Europe. But the worst misery of all came from the north, from the Viking raids of the pagan Northmen. That obscure wanderlust common to all Germanic tribes drove the Viking long-boats out of the fjords some years before the turn of the ninth century; in 793 a blazing monastery on the Northumbrian coast of

England was the first alarm-beacon of their coming. For the next century the sinister ships lined with shields spread steadily through Europe. Every river mouth in Europe was a welcoming doorway to plunder. By way of the Ouse they reached York, by the Thames and lesser streams they came to Reading. The Rhine led to Cologne, the Scheldt to Cambrai, the Seine to Paris, the Loire to Fleury. Farm and village and town were in equal danger from them; by 890 York, London, Cologne, Rouen, Nantes, Paris, Orleans, Bordeaux and many smaller cities had been successfully assaulted. Neither distance nor difficulty deterred the Vikings. Hacked limbs, eviscerated animals, burning houses, a jumble of loot carelessly abandoned by some safe anchorage marked their crimson progress to the western coast of Spain, to the islands of the Mediterranean, to Italy and Sicily, to the heart of Russia, and from there down the rivers that lead to the Black Sea and Constantinople. Nor did they stop where the waters ended. Very soon they learnt to round up horses at the end of rivers and raid the inland country. Lamentations in the litanies of the western Church gave witness to their appalling effect: 'From the savage nation of the Northmen, which lays waste our realm, O

St Edmund, the English king, led into captivity by the Danes. From the *Life and Miracles of St Edmund*, 12th Cent.

Lord deliver us.' Princes and abbots, attempting to buy them off with regular payments, only encouraged a speedy return. Yet to stand against them was to invite certain slaughter. Glorying in war-like deeds, they went forward remorselessly, tirelessly and without pity. The saga tells of a Viking scornfully called the 'children's man' because he would not impale babes on his lance 'as was the custom of his fellows'. And to this already fearful brutality there was added a further orgiastic ferocity induced by drugs or drink. In 1012, the Archbishop of Canterbury, captured and kept for ransom, was suddenly set on at a banquet and beaten to death by bones thrown at him from the feasting-tables.

In the many terrible years before the wandering invaders of the outer lands were incorporated into the more peaceful body of Europe, the settled kingdoms of the west had two sources of strength to meet the invasions. First, they had the patient teachings of Christianity, and the civil traditions of Rome which had themselves been inherited through conquest. In time all in the west were tamed by these gentle forces, became Christian, tilled the land, built cities, studied letters, ordained laws, traded instead of plundered. But second, they felt also the wilder urgings of their own Teutonic blood, and remembered their descent from martial races bound by oaths and blood-bonds to the pursuit of military glory. In the early despair brought on by invasion, with concerted defence impossible to organize, each knight naturally answered the call of blood, took arms and horse as his fathers had done and set out in an individual fury to make a more thorough desert of desolation. Countries groaned with the universal cry of all peaceful folk caught inexorably between invaders and defenders: 'Our property went in plunder, and our hopes were in vain. Our affairs were in anarchy, and muttering together was our only counsel. They drove away our beasts and led off our horses under burdens that crushed their saddles, with loads of furniture, clothing, money and goods, both what was in use and what was stored. To this hath Fate condemned some of her people. The calamities of some appear a feast to others.'

Under frequent raids towns dwindled into forlorn villages. Tilled fields became wastes, trodden down or burnt by this side or that, as the English, attempting to relieve Chester from a Viking attack in 894, 'carried off all the cattle round about, burned the harvests and caused the whole of the surrounding countryside to be eaten up by their horses'. King Alfred sadly looked back to a time in England 'before everything was ravaged and burned, when the churches of England overflowed with treasures and with books'. Wind sighed across empty villages, in and out of ruined monasteries; agriculture declined, new land was not cleared, old land was blighted and went to seed. Lights of civilization dimmed. Northumbria, homeland of Bede, the school that sent the monk Alcuin to be tutor, friend and adviser to Charlemagne, became once more a land of rocks and ruins and wild weather. 'To yield is to become the barbarian's slave; to fight is to cast our bones on the waste ground.'

But fighting was the only proper business of knightly nobles, bred out of the old *comitatus*. As in all times when civil arts are in decay, once again military prowess seemed the only worthwhile virtue. Continuous struggle engendered a lust for war; and the sternness of the contest demanded ferocity and anger equal to those of the invaders. They became the ordinary qualities of knighthood faithfully recorded without surprise in the old epic poetry of Europe.

On 15th August 778, a force of Basques caught and destroyed the rear-guard of Charlemagne's army in the passes of the Pyrenees, killing a certain Rolandus and a great many Franks. Legend has transformed the Basques into Saracens and the little-known Rolandus, Count of the Breton Marches, into Roland, pre-eminent champion of Christendom and renowned hero of the *Chanson de Roland*. Folk-memory and the wiles of the poet have given a short, blood-stained tumult the graces of epic action. Brave armies advance in the bright sun. The Saracens ride out, sparkling in triple layers of chain, with banners of crimson, white and blue held high; light flashes on arms and harness; a thousand trumpets bray out their challenge. And to meet them Roland rides from the mountain pass, so debonair astride his charger Veillantif and with the good sword Durendal by his hand. The white battle-pennant waves from the uplifted point of his lance; his pace at the head of the Frankish line is firm, slow, relentless, but his face is bright with laughter. Noble words are spoken, and great deeds are done before the cold moon shines on the bodies of the vanquished Franks.

Behind the epic bravery lies another reality, a harsher world of treachery and cunning, pride and selfishness, cruelty and blood-lust. No knight is to be trusted; not even Charlemagne can control the selfish rage of his favourite nobles. Spite and jealousy are the chief spurs to action; a fantastical and closely guarded 'honour' is best satisfied by spoil and slaughter. Charlemagne sits joyfully in the captured Saracen town, his baggage-train swollen with enormous booty, the defeated inhabitants forcibly converted to Christianity or summarily executed. Ganelon, stepfather of the hero Roland, betrays the Franks and sends his stepson to a certain death. Turpin, archbishop of the Christian host, does such deeds of blood, they would astound a savage: 'The archbishop's crozier has a mighty power,' says the poet with innocent admiration. As for Roland himself, pride begins his downfall, for he will not sound the horn to summon Charlemagne to his aid. 'That would be mad,' he tells the apprehensive Oliver. 'For I would lose renown throughout sweet France.' Quarrelling, the 'dear companions' Oliver and Roland ride to battle, to meet the consequence of foolhardy pride in a black fury of slaughter. Oliver, lanced through the back, rages like a beast deprived of vengeance, cutting through spears and shields, hacking off hands and feet, slicing through men, harness and horses, and tossing dismembered bodies in heaps. Roland, overcome by grief and wounds and baffled pride, near death since 'his brains are seeping out of both his ears', makes a last assault, attempts to break his faithful sword, then puts sword and horn by his side under a pine, turns his face towards Spain and dies amid carnage. Blood everywhere: the living arm-deep in gore, with hauberk and horses spat-

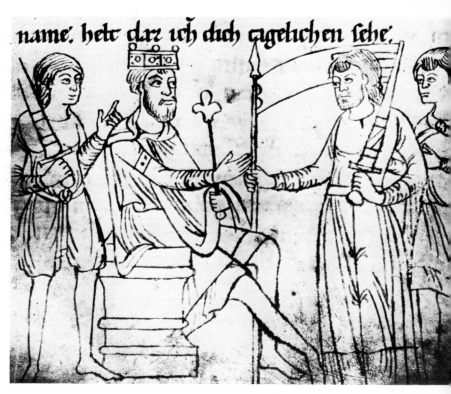

name. het daz ich dich agelichen sehe.

Charlemagne invests Roland as lord of the Spanish March. From a 12th Cent manuscript.

tered crimson; the dead cut in pieces, pierced through shield and armour down to the very bone. Few words of remorse, less of pity, but chiefly 'Bright blood spread about on every hand: On the green grass bright red blood flows down.'

Pride, foolhardiness, greed, shameless brutality: these are the authentic lineaments of early western knighthood, however cloaked in the epic by the rich tapestry of heroic imagination. Infidels and pagans might be butchered with an easy conscience; but the epics of Christian quarrels show the same instincts and conduct at work. Some time in 943 the sons of Herbert de Vermandois had their territory invaded by Raoul, son of Raoul de Gouy. The invaders were driven off and killed, and this obscure feudal brawl was given a fanciful poetic form in *Raoul de Cambrai*. The progress of this Christian is like a storm of passion bordering on insanity. 'Take arms in haste,' he cries; 'four hundred of you ride speedily and reach Origny before night-fall. Spread my tent in the middle of the church; let my pack-horses be tethered in the porches; prepare my food beneath the vaults, fasten my falcons on the golden crosses and make ready a rich bed before the altar where I may lie. I will lean against the crucifix and deliver the nuns up to my squires. I mean to destroy the place and ruin it utterly because the sons of Herbert hold it so dear.' This poem of knighthood reveals Raoul as the despoiler of churches, the murderer of nuns, the rebellious vassal of the King, and the merciless destroyer of all opposition, young, old, sick or wounded. Like some rabid animal, Raoul must at last be put down by his own reluctant liegeman. 'By God, Raoul,' groans one of his victims, 'now thou art no better than a heathen, for thou art proud and wicked and full of presumption. Now thou seemest no better to me than a mad dog, since thou deniest God and his love.' What Raoul is, so too are most other knights in the poem: old Guerri, a white-bearded warlock never satiated with blood; the sons of Vermandois and the champions of Cambrai in angry turbulence, scratching out quarrels as frantic as jackals; young Gautier, the inheritor of Raoul's blood-feud, and no less relentless and bloodthirsty. Neither love nor mercy nor faith nor loyalty can restrain the inhuman passions of warriors roused for battle. Primitive blood, in subjection to fierce northern gods, bursts all bounds of sense, all measure of control.

Under the shadow of the sword, a kneeling man puts his hands between those of another, offering submission in return for protection. They rise and kiss, symbolizing eternal friendship. Thus was homage done in the old Germanic way, and the feudal bond tied between man and master. Later, perhaps in the Carolingian age, a new element was added; an oath of faith, or 'fealty', was taken on relics or the Gospel, giving Christian blessing to the old rite.

Ties based on personal dependence and loyalty were not rare in the old Teutonic world; every chief worthy of the name, as Tacitus commented, had his band of personal 'men'. Time, blending elements of Germanic custom with remnants of Roman law and tradition, instilled in Europe a complex world of dependencies, from slave to king. This drift towards feudalism was given a violent impetus by the invasions, particularly by the inroads of the Northmen. To be unprotected invited death or continual flight; each rank in society eagerly sought to place itself under the patronage of one above—the lower ranks for their very survival, the higher ranks in the interest of greater strength and security. And looking downwards from top to bottom, the king needed vassals to raise an army, and the nobles needed 'clients' to make up the bands they were committed to provide the king. Necessity and self-interest intermingled. Fear or poverty was enough to make very many offer themselves in voluntary 'commendation'; and if those forces were not sufficient, the greater man in search of power drove lesser men into submission by blackmail and intimidation. A man with a strong master was well protected; a lord with numerous dependents was powerful indeed.

The insecurity of warring lands brought feudalism to its full flowering. But the burdens of war were expensive and time-consuming. Levies of raw peasants with no other arms than stones and farm implements were of little use. The cavalry had been proved the men to win battles so that horsemen were encouraged almost to the exclusion of any infantry at all. The Franks had started as foot-soldiers; yet in 891 a chronicler noted the Frankish reluctance to storm a palisade at Louvain 'because it was not usual for the nobles of the Franks to fight on foot'. Charles the Bald boasted that his cavalry army was so great, 'their horses would drink up the Rhine, so that he might go over dry-shod'. Heavy cavalry became the very core of military power. Even the Northmen, finally contained by the French knights, took to horses when they settled in Normandy and formed the squadrons that Duke William led to England in 1066.

But few could afford the equipment of cavalry. By the Ripuarian Law a horse was worth six cows, a satisfactory cuirass with metal plates was worth the same, and even a helmet cost three cows. Moreover, the training of a proficient horse-soldier was long and difficult. 'You can make a horseman of a lad by puberty,' said a wise proverb; 'later than that, never.'

Leisure, long training and wealth were the making of cavalry. And since the dangers of the age demanded cavalry, feudalism encouraged and perpetuated a leisured and wealthy class dedicated, almost with the solemnity of a priesthood, to warfare. The members of this class were the noble knights, the *bellatores* of society, who fought while the *oratores* prayed, and the *laboratores* supported all with the labour of their hands. 'The work of the clerk is to pray to God,' says an old French poem, 'and of the knight to do justice, while the labourer finds their bread. One labours, one prays, and another defends. In the field, in the town, in the church these three help one another according to right order.' This elegant arrangement, said the thirteenth-century *Image du Monde*, was approved by all sensible people from the earliest times; Greek philosophers had taught it to the Romans, who had passed it on to the French. The lord, so the theory went, had the onerous task of defeating enemies and maintaining justice, and therefore well-deserved his privileges: 'The people come before lords; but it is the numerous small folk who wish for peace, and create lords to restrain and defeat the strong and to give each man his rights, so that each may live according to his condition, the poor with their poverty and the rich with their riches.'

Those who become necessary naturally become honoured. The 'knight' (the trained horseman who guarded the land) in feudal times became 'noble'. Arab historians of the crusades were surprised by the honour done to fighting-men. 'Among the Franks (God damn them!) no quality is more highly esteemed in a man than military prowess.' wrote Usama ibn Munqidh. 'The knights have a monopoly of the positions of honour and importance among them, and no one else has any prestige in their eyes. They are the men who give counsel, pass judgment, and command the armies.'

But the elevation of the warrior to the front rank of society was also a silent glorification of war. Free from the rude forces of the market-place, his economic well-being supported on the sweaty backs of villeins, the feudal knight indulged the only qualities he had in the only business he knew. Born and trained for nothing but fighting, he embraced war with the passion of a lover. Bertran de Born, knight and troubadour, celebrated the violent rites of his kind: 'I love to see, amid the meadows, tents and pavilions spread; with joy I see knights and horses drawn up on the field in battle array; and it delights me when peasants and herds scatter before the scouts, with a great body of men-at-arms following; and my heart is filled with gladness when I see strong castles besieged, and the walls broken and overwhelmed, and the warriors on the bank, among ditches and strong lines of interwoven stakes.' And from the bravery of the field

The artist of this Latin Bible has portrayed biblical warfare according to 11th Cent usage. The chief battle is undertaken by bands of heavy cavalry, very well defended by enveloping chain-mail, conical helmets and round bucklers, and relying for offence on the long lance or spear. At this stage in the fight the swords still rest in the scabbards.

the knightly heart passes with a quickening pulse to the energy of the fight: 'Maces, swords, helms of different colours, shields that will be split and shattered in the fight; many vassals struck down together; and the horses of the dead and wounded wandering at will. And when the battle is joined, let all noble men think of nothing but the breaking of heads and arms; for it is better to die than to be vanquished and live. I tell you, food and wine and sleep are not so dear to me as the shouts of On, On! from both sides, and the neighing of steeds that have lost their riders, and the cries of Help, Help!; as the sight of men great and small falling to the grass beyond the ditches; as the sight, at last, of the dead with the broken lance, pennant still fluttering, sticking out of the side.'

The honour paid to the knight helped to perpetuate his ugly qualities. His high place in feudal society sanctified his barbarity—at least in his own eyes—and made him almost ungovernable. There he was, in time of peace, immured in his fortified house, assailed by draughts and stench and smoke, fretted by the irritations of domesticity and the puzzlements of his own invincible ignorance, with little but hunting and feasting to fill the weary days. He was one, said the *Chanson de Guillaume*, who ate the haunch of a boar at a sitting and tossed down a gallon of wine in a couple of gulps: 'Pity the man on whom he wages war!' To war he was inevitably driven, as much by boredom and stupidity as by the pursuit of honour and the hope of gain. With what relief he took the shield from the hook, polished sword and lance, dusted the cuirass and shook the moths from the hauberk, shod and bridled the war-horse, and saying good-bye to his castle of dirt and dullness set out lightly, with his mounted squire by his side, to meet his liegemen and go in search of any affray. He was, as William the Conqueror complained of an errant vassal, 'unsteady and extravagant, spending his time gadding from place to place'.

Monarchs and ministers might well complain, for the conduct of remote vassals was never predictable. Feudal loyalties were at heart the ancient blood-loyalties of the family or kindred group, and a knight who might easily and willingly die in defence of his immediate lord, might not cross the road on the order of a distant king. 'Here we must stand in duty to our king,' said Roland on the field of Roncesvalles: 'A man should suffer greatly for his lord, Accept the heat, withstand the bitter cold And, as his duty, lose both hide and hair.' But those who were not the king's 'men' directly cared little for the king's word if it went against the interests of their kindred. In *Raoul de Cambrai*, Guerri the Red, a most intrepid warmonger, roundly insults the weak king who tries to disentangle the feudal vendetta. 'Just emperor,' he cries, curiously mixing formal salutation with undisguised contempt, 'a great folly has been committed here. By God, you are not worth a fig, O king. How could I look at that vile traitor who treacherously slew my nephew?' Yet the same Guerri, this hard-hearted monster, weeps unrestrainedly at the loss of his own vassals, killed in the violence he has so furiously promoted: 'Guerri looks around and sees his vassals lying dead and bleeding and he is overcome with grief. With his right hand he makes the sign of the cross over them and says, "Alas for you, my noble knights of Cambrai, for you are beyond my aid".' Such was a poet's account of the overriding strength of blood-ties among feudal knights. And the evidence of history merely confirms the poet's view. In 1250, when St Louis's unruly crusaders were being thoroughly rattled at Mansura in Egypt, the historian Joinville singled out for praise the efforts of Guy Mauvoisin. 'He and his won great honour from that day's work,' wrote Joinville; 'and it is not to be wondered at that they bore themselves well, for I was told by those who were well acquainted with his dispositions that almost all his company was made up of knights who were of his own kin or his liegemen.' Personal pride and family honour meant much more than such abstract notions as the good of the country or the security of the state. A noble of Périgord, in the twelfth century, devastated the countryside to avenge an insult to his looks; he and his fellow knights considered with equanimity the presence of Anglo-Norman intruders in the land of France. Raoul of Cambrai could not be dissuaded from his barren feud, for 'everyone would say that I was afraid, and my heirs would be disgraced forever'.

Kings might complain of the pride, indiscipline and selfishness of knights; merchants and townsmen had more practical reasons to fear their infinite rapacity. Knightly honour walked a crooked road; the keenest mind would be hard put to decide warfare from brigand-

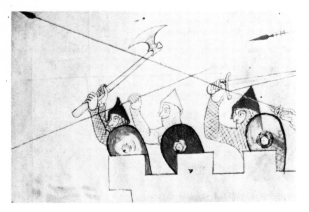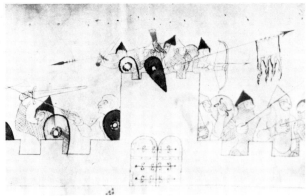

Knights fighting, at the end of the
11th Cent. Knights in the usual
surcoat of chain-mail, with the early
conical helmet, defend the
battlements with battle-axe, sword,
spear and bow. The bow is smaller
than the later, powerful English
longbow, and seems to be drawn to
the breast only. From the Bible of
St Etienne, 1109.

age. How easy it was in lawless times to call thefts 'requisitions',
and to make 'reprisals' the excuse for a general piracy. Bertran de
Born expressed this morality with his usual blunt force: 'Soon we
shall see trumpets, drums, flags and pennons, standards and horses.
And that will be a happy day, for we shall seize the usurers' goods;
no longer shall pack-animals go safely by day, nor shall the townsmen
journey without fear, nor the merchant on his way to France. But
the man who is full of courage shall be rich.' In the poem *Girart de
Roussillon* the hero, outlawed and incognito, pretends to a group of
merchants that Girart is dead. 'God be praised,' the merchants
reply, 'for he was a warmonger and a danger to our lives and our
trade.' Then the knightly face grew dark, and but for the lack of a
sword he would have killed one or two. When Richard the Lionheart
was asked to release his prisoner Philippe de Dreux, Bishop of
Beauvais, he replied that the man he had captured had appeared as a
knight in full armour, 'a robber, a tyrant, an incendiary who inces-
santly devastated the land'. Plunder was the recognized and desirable
profit of feudal war, and merchants were merely the victims of
familiar events.

But the laments of ministers and merchants against the knights
were only whispers compared with the groans of the poor. 'We must
hold our men dear,' says one good-hearted and truthful poet, 'for
villeins carry the burden of us all, whether we are knights, clerks
or ladies.' But how were they treated in reality? Jacques de Vitry gave
this picture: 'All that the peasant gathers in a year of stubborn work,
the noble knight devours in an hour. Not content with the wages of
war, not content with his revenues and taxes, he further despoils his
subjects by heavy demands and illegal extortions. The poor are
exhausted, the fruits of their pain and sorrow are wrested from them.'

Quite naturally, for such was the destiny allotted to them by their
feudal betters, the poor were the chief victims of the knight's
brutality. In war, the peasants of the levies formed an unwieldy
bulk, mere *pedones*, plodding infantrymen, rustically armed, inept
and liable to panic. In any estimation of military power they counted
for nothing, they were so easily cut down by the prancing cavalry.
After the battle, *Girart de Roussillon* tells us with the ring of a grim
truth, the captured knights were preserved for ransoming while
men of no account were casually slaughtered. We see at the taking of

Jerusalem, in the summer of 1099, western knights gathering up great numbers of the enemy, as was their habit, 'either killing them or taking them captive'. To avoid them, very many Saracens took refuge on the roof of the Temple where the knights typically and stealthily followed them; 'some of our men', said the *Gesta Francorum*, 'cautiously ascended to the roof of the Temple and attacked the Saracens, both men and women, beheading them with naked swords; the remainder sought death by jumping from the Temple.'

And when the poor were released from the dangers of war, they were still the sufferers in a peace so often made hazardous by feuding knights. The reign of Stephen in England was a demonstration of all that was bad and fearful in a land of grasping, unrestrained

Warfare of the 12th Cent: the attackers use crossbow, the ordinary bow, and a trebuchet, or catapult, operated by manpower; the defenders reply with a similar catapult. From *De rebus siculis carmen* by Peter of Eboli.

feudal knights. In the whole country, the *Chronicle of Ramsey* lamented, force triumphed over reason. And the *Historia Eliensis*, speaking of the hell-bent career of the treacherous knight Geoffrey de Mandeville, recounted some of the effects of force. In a space of twenty or thirty miles neither ox nor plough could be seen, and a bushel of grain rose to two hundred pence. Starvation killed the poor by the hundreds, and their bodies lay in the fields unburied, carrion for birds and beasts. A sulphurous yellow light from flaming villages poisoned the night sky; chains of captives stumbled on ravaged roads;

women and children were killed out of hand; instruments of torture squeezed ransom money from tormented bodies. 'In the screams of the afflicted, men saw the fulfilment of the words of St John the Apostle, "Men shall wish to die and death shall flee from them".'

And the terror that Mandeville inflicted on the fenlands of Ely was (according to the *Anglo-Saxon Chronicle*) merely a part of the general woe. Robber-barons stalked the land in search of any prey, and when they caught their victims 'no martyrs were ever so tortured as they were'. They were hung by the thumbs, or tourniquets were twisted about the head until they cut into the brain; they were put in dungeons with snakes, or crushed in small chests under great stones; they were fastened in spiked collars so that they could neither sit nor lie nor sleep. The knights took protection-money until the villagers could pay no more, and then they burnt the village, 'so that you could easily go a whole day's journey and never find an occupied village, nor tilled land. Then corn was dear, and meat and butter and cheese, because there was none in the country.' For nineteen years these trials persisted, 'and men said openly that Christ and his saints slept'.

At the turn of the millennium the conditions were passing that had led to the rise of feudal cavalry. The great invasions had ceased, and nations were settling with established borders. The knight had

Vice and virtue, from carving on a capital in Clermont-Ferrand, represented by two fully armed knights of the 12th Cent.

done his work well and proved the superiority of the heavy horseman. The victory at Hastings in 1066 put the final stamp of triumph on his labours, the mercenary mounted knights of Duke William, serving 'some for land and some for pence', only just overcoming the resolute housecarls of Harold and the native levies of the English fyrd, who all fought on foot. The result was indeed a desperate near thing, and this sternly-fought contest by the hoar-apple tree on Senlac Hill was a lesson and an omen. The cruel ravages of the Norman knights at their first landings in Kent and Sussex, a barbarousness which greatly stiffened the resistance of Harold's army, taught England what to expect from uncontrolled feudal nobles. And the cloud of arrows which pierced Harold in the eye, and at last determined the day, might have warned the knights of their fallibility; for just as the importation of stirrup and horseshoe was the making of heavy cavalry, so the improvement of archery (in particular the power of the long-bow) was the undoing of that same cavalry. But for the moment, the battle of Hastings, which set up an enduring Norman dynasty in England, was the last successful occasion of feudal power.

His work done, the feudal knight (so restless and irritable, so proud and undisciplined, so brave and ignorant) became nothing but a force for disruption and evil. Long before the First Crusade his reputation preceded him to the east. Anna Comnena wrote that her

A Norman knight, descendant of the Vikings, one of the type that contested the Battle of Hastings. Arms and armour had changed little in two hundred years, but the kite-shaped shield was now preferred to the round buckler. Detail from a 12th Cent capital in Monreale, Sicily.

father, the Byzantine Emperor, viewed the approach of the westerners with apprehension: 'He feared the incursions of these people, for he had already experienced the savage fury of their attack, their fickleness of mind, and their readiness to approach anything with violence.' The evidence of the feudal west gave the Emperor Alexius good reason for his fears. He saw division and jealousy everywhere: countries split into provinces, those into seigneuries, those into lesser fiefs, and all contending in a virulent

The German Emperor Henry VI and his knights during an Italian campaign. This illustration, from a poem by Peter of Eboli which is a testament to the warring anarchy of the 12th Cent, shows that the armed horseman was evolving into the chevalier, bearing the insignia and heraldic devices typical of chivalry.

hatred. He saw almost every petty nobleman shut in the security of his fortified house, casting baleful eyes over the countryside, and issuing forth from time to time in acts of rebellion or robbery. Warring vassals reduced life to the simple equation of the jungle, predator or victim, snarling from their castles as from a lair built (as one contemporary explained) 'to enable these men, always occupied with quarrels and massacres, to protect themselves from their enemies, to triumph over their equals, to oppress their inferiors'. Too often a knight was a terror to the people, a danger to kings, an embarrassment to the Church. Who could tame this fractious and malevolent beast?

# chapter two

There was, men knew well, war in heaven, and the hope to avoid it in this plain of infirmities was illusory. St Augustine, forever watchful of human failings and living at the time when the Vandals raised the ashes of the empire, found war the certain inheritance of our misery. 'What is there to condemn in war? Is it the death of men who must sooner or later die? I declare that this reproach comes from the mouths of cowards, and should not be made among truly religious men.' Without the sanction of a greater force, the wicked went unchecked and prospered by their deeds. 'Such crimes must be punished,' wrote Augustine, expounding the judgment of a righteous war, 'and that is the reason why, according to God's commands and by lawful authority, good people are compelled to engage in certain wars.'

In the twilight days of the barbaric invasions the strong pessimism of Augustine, the most powerful voice of early Christianity, had a more than natural appeal. No wonder it became a fundamental duty of the great feudal lord or king to wage the righteous war. And this was naturally seen as part of his prime care, to protect the true faith and ensure the salvation of his people. War, which looked immediately so senseless, bestial and selfish, could not be divorced, in a larger signification, from the duties of faith. The feudal warrior was never at rest, and his stained sword hardly ever in its sheath. But observe the tumult of the angels in heaven, wrote the theorist Honoré Bonet in his fourteenth-century *Tree of Battles*, and 'hence it is no great marvel if in this world there arise wars and battles, since they existed first in heaven'.

But a heavenly precedent was no licence for terrestrial savagery. The Church, which reluctantly countenanced just wars, none the less had a duty to condemn and try to limit the bestial appetites stirred up in battle. 'What is blameworthy', wrote St Augustine, is not the necessity to fight but 'the desire to hurt other men and the cruel love of vengeance. It is this implacable spirit, this enemy of peace, this savagery of revolt, this passion for domination and empire.' The biblical text was clear: those that live by the sword shall die by the sword. And the Church fathers and the early popes had been steady in their condemnation of violent men. 'He who can think of war and bear the thought without great sorrow', Augustine lamented, 'is indeed a man dead to human feelings.'

Exhortation was not enough, for the action of the clergy, specially in the feudal age, seemed quite contrary to the words of the fathers. Churchmen were not exempt from feudal ties. Abbots and bishops, all owners of great estates, were charged to provide their armed levies in time of trouble, and many a bold priest rode to battle at the

A monk-knight, from a carving in the cloisters at Conques. Because the Church intervened in all aspects of life, and also tried to regulate martial passion, fighting churchmen were familiar figures in the Middle Ages.

head of his battalion. Turpin, the fighting Archbishop of the *Chanson de Roland*, was no mere figure of fancy. Many an historical prelate fought as vigorously and died as violently. Geoffrey, Bishop of Coutances, and Odo, Bishop of Bayeux, half-brother of the Conqueror, both stood in William's ranks at Hastings. In a lower place, the Almoner of Fécamp led the knights that owed allegiance to his Abbot. At a later date, the bishops of Châlons, Sens and Melun disputed the day at Poitiers, and the Archbishop of Sens was killed on the field at Agincourt. These were the more respectable of the church-warriors. Some were no better than bandits. The palace of Hugh de Noyers, rebellious Bishop of Auxerre, was more a military stronghold than a house of religion, 'surrounded by wide ditches, bordered by great palisades, and dominated by a donjon with ramparts, turrets and a drawbridge'. Philippe de Dreux, robber Bishop of Beauvais, rode through the lands of Richard Lionheart, burning, looting and killing.

Because the worst churchmen welcomed war, and the best were unafraid of it (even the saintly Abbot Suger of Saint-Denis called on the French King to put down the nobles of the Île-de-France), the Church knew very well, and at first hand, the excesses of the feudal knight. A few priests, corrupted by the familiar evils of power-lust and greed, sank as low as the worst knights. But most saw the heartache of petty fiefdoms always at war, and heard the mutterings of good people praying for peace.

Kings, with their limited feudal power and their empty purses, were unable to give their dominions the blessing of quiet. Nor were they, in most cases, the men to talk of peace, though they knew the benefit of a peaceful kingdom. King Canute, who desperately (but hopelessly) enacted a law for troublesome England that all men over twelve 'shall swear never to rob or become the accomplice of a robber', was himself a robber Viking at heart of whom the poets sang that 'the blazing dwellings of men lit the path of thy advance'. We read in Ordericus Vitalis that the politic Henry I of England ordered the blinding of his own grand-daughters as a retribution on a son-in-law, who had put out the eyes of a royal servant. Words of peace came more persuasively from the mouth of the Church than from the lips of such kings.

In all meetings of men the talk was of war and death and violence. The bad news was the pre-occupation of bishops as well as kings. At Charroux, about the year 989, a council of bishops tentatively began to impose the Church's formal limit on violence, anathematizing those who broke open churches, stole from the peasants, or struck an unarmed cleric. This was the beginnings of the *Pax Dei*, the Peace of God which exempted certain people or things from the customary brigandage. A synod of Le Puy, in 990, extended the protection to merchants and gave more detailed prohibitions against destroying a mill, or uprooting vines. The movement spread and became a kind of feudal pact administered under oath, which many none the less refused to join. The pact agreed on at Beauvais in 1023 was typical, protecting churches and clergy, limiting the violence done to peasants, and safeguarding as much as possible their beasts and livestock. The aims of the *Pax Dei* were modest enough; some pacts allowed the stealing of cattle as necessary food for a war-party, and other lords promised 'I will not kill the villeins' beasts, except on my own land'. The right to prosecute the blood-feud after a

Troubles of feudal times: the burning of a town. The strange, dog-headed helmets of the soldiers lend a suitable impression of evil to the event. From the *Chroniques de France*, 14th Cent.

murder was nearly always permitted. The intention was merely to write the rules of warfare more strictly, and to keep the innocent by-standers outside the field of action.

As protection was given to certain things, so by a simple extension of thought peace was enjoined on certain days. The *Truga Dei*, the Truce of God, ordained a closed season for private wars. A capitulary of Charlemagne had forbidden the carrying on of blood-feuds on a Sunday. In 1027, a local synod meeting in a Toulonges meadow revived the order. The day's respite was a reminder of the almost forgotten joys of peace, and soon Easter was added to the forbidden days. By 1041 the Truce of God had, in theory, a good hold on the week, extending from Wednesday night until the end of Sunday: as the Council of Nice explained, Thursday was sacred to the Ascension, Friday to the Passion, Saturday to the Adoration, and Sunday to the Resurrection. Later orders banned private wars from Advent to Epiphany, from Septuagesima to Easter, and placed under the Truce the Feast of the Virgin and those of various saints. Those who wished to make war and keep the Truce had to hurry indeed; consequently the prohibitions were generally neglected.

The Church's first attempt to govern war was not a great success. Many feudal knights would have no part of these pacts, reluctant to give up their rough but agreeable life of terrorism. Many of the clergy thought it no business of priests to meddle in the secular affairs of lords. And ingrained habits were hard to erase, even among those of good intentions. When Bishop Guy of Le Puy assembled his

knights and villeins in 990 and 'besought them to pledge themselves by oath to keep the peace, not to oppress the churches or the poor, and to give back what they had carried off', his hearers simply refused. The good Bishop then felt an honest upsurge of angry blood, gathered his troops by night, and in the morning 'set out to force the recalcitrants to take the oath of peace and give hostages: which, with the help of God, was done'. Such intrepid acts were a queer preparation for peace. In 1038 Archbishop Aimon of Bourges constituted a peasant militia which marched under parochial banners against the strongholds of robber-barons. Several castles were reduced by this fervent army, whose artillery hurled rocks and whose poor cavalry jogged on donkeys, until the lord of Déols caught and massacred the 'peacemakers' on the banks of the Cher. Other brotherhoods of peasants or townsmen appeared, some guided by visions, and in the name of peace brought several regions to the verge of civil war. For the sake of proper order and for the sanctity of old institutions, bishops and nobles and robber barons felt it wise to combine against these upstart levies. Neither Church nor State could accept the *Pax Dei* as a cover for the overthrow of established social order.

'Gladly the lance becomes a scythe, gladly the sword turns to a ploughshare. Peace enriches the poor, brings down the proud.' Thus

*Left.* The sanctuary of the church gave a refuge to peasants against the tyranny of the knights. In this carving from St Nectaire, a peasant clings to a church pillar while a knight tries to drag him away by the hair and a churchman, with drawn sword, tries to pull the man away from the knight.

Armed peasants of the 11th Cent. Rural bands of this kind, armed very often with weapons more primitive than those shown here, collected together chiefly to resist the violence of feudal knights. Illustration from a late 11th Cent psalter.

Fulbert of Rheims prematurely sang, at the start of the eleventh century. That fortunate time was not yet, but the wisdom of the Church was now set against the rule of the anarchic knight. Ungovernable by temperament and conviction, the feudal knight was still susceptible, in his unlettered ignorance, to the primitive idealism of Christendom. Had not the Church, administering the oath of fealty over relics of the saints, consecrated the knight in his feudal place? Had not the campaigns of the knight against the various barbarians been undertaken in defence of the faith? Whatever his luxurious sins, the knight dimly intuited that he was a member of the Christian commonwealth, and not the least member either considering his important service against invading pagans. Though he could not be ordered to keep the peace, he might be subtly reformed—at least turned towards more honourable warfare—if only the Church could enlist his prowess in some task affecting the Christian conscience.

In the last quarter of the eleventh century the Seljuq Turks overran Palestine and took Jerusalem. These uncouth warriors from the steppes, Moslems but as yet untamed by Islam, made Christian life in Jerusalem almost impossible; pilgrims were killed, robbed or driven back, and the holy places were maltreated. 'The navel of the world', the west lamented, was in cruel, impious hands: 'base and bastard Turks hold sway over our brothers.' A resurgent papacy called for Christian arms, and a great work of reconquest was pointed out to soldiers of faith. In answer to this call, by imperceptible workings of idealism, armed horsemen turned into chevaliers, and feudal brawlers into chivalric knights.

To Clermont, in Auvergne, came Pope Urban II in a cold November, to consider with his Council of abbots and bishops the state of Christendom. He saw, wrote the chronicler, the Church degraded, peace despised, and the princes in perpetual strife. 'He saw the goods of the land stolen from the owners; and many, who were unjustly taken captive and most barbarously cast into foul prisons, he saw ransomed for excessive sums, or tormented there by the three evils, starvation, thirst and cold, or allowed to perish by unseen death. He saw also holy places violated, monasteries and villas destroyed by fire, and not a little human suffering, both the divine and the human being held in derision.' In anger he saw Jerusalem denied to Christians; in compassion he considered the plight of the Holy Land. On 27th November 1095, in a wan light, the Pope in the winter of his life put on the dignity of office and began: 'Dearest brethren, I, Urban, invested by the permission of God with the papal tiara, and spiritual ruler over the whole world, have come here in this great crisis to you, servants of God, as a messenger of divine admonition.'

Four accounts remain of that strange admonition by which a pope, out of desperation at his own insufficiency and lack of power, infected the whole mind of Europe. The simple patriot Robert the Monk saw the Franks expressly summoned, as the race chosen and beloved by God, to banish unclean nations from the Holy Places:

*Opposite, top.* Attacks on the west: Constantinople, at the limit of western territory, was constantly under pressure from the eastern lands beyond. From a Greek manuscript of the 12th Cent.

*Opposite, bottom.* Nomad Bulgarian and Hungarian horsemen attacking the settled towns of the west. From a Greek manuscript of the 12th Cent.

λο ιο καιαποπολεμου· αλλαπανταλαφρουκεπειπει· αμπεκε]τογαρκωνπαντηροσγηπε
πωνυμιαγλειχρυδης· ταπρωτατοτε παραβασιλεωσοφρων καιμεγαπαρατουτοσθψαμενος
Καιπησκουλησ ταυτησυπαρχοντων· Οθελθοντωνδε τουτωνπαριδηλινοτιαν· ωσαρκοστι
ραμμοσ· ταπαμβαν τουκαποπλισαοθψαμεσ· επεισιπιβαρβαυρκομεγαλωσ· Καιπαπωρικλεφοσθηντα
φρονιδιαπεμψων· τρεπσειβατουσερδον·

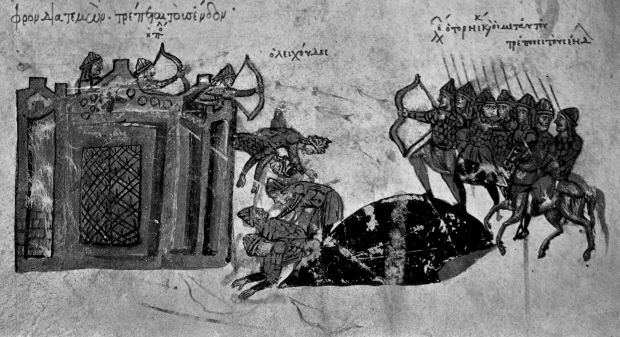

Νικησαμψεθσαιοιτουρκοι· ητησαμψοτομιασολεατοιω καταοχεθεντασ· πολιπεμψαρμησαμβα
προσδεκαταρδασ· τοιπολιτασθαωφτε]λενειστηντουπεμωσ Σψμψεν· θρασιδεισων
οσυμεων· διαποδρουγαρουαδγθουτον καθολεαμ ακενενεαριτσειρημτε· προσημ πωιξεβε
οπασλασ· καιτουχλφοσφακτηνλεοντα]ιωπωπωκαθσαλεξαπεθσελεταθ αοπρωδη· Και

'Oh, most valiant soldiers and descendants of invincible ancestors, be not degenerate, but recall the valour of your forefathers.' Balderic recorded a more universal appeal, vigorously brought home to the shameful knights of the western world: 'Listen and learn!' cried out the inspired Pope. 'You, girt about with the badge of knighthood, are arrogant with great pride; you rage against your brothers and cut each other in pieces. The true soldiery of Christ does not rend asunder the sheepfold of the Redeemer. The Holy Church has reserved a soldiery for herself to help her people, but you debase

Pictures from the *Roman de Godefroi de Bouillon* illustrating the events leading to the First Crusade. (*Left*) Pope Urban II arrives in France, and (*right*) he preaches to the Church dignatories at Clermont.

her wickedly to her hurt. Let us confess the truth, whose heralds we ought to be; truly, you are not holding to the way that leads to life. You, the oppressors of children, plunderers of widows; you guilty of homicide, of sacrilege, robbers of others' rights; you who await the pay of thieves for the shedding of Christian blood—as vultures smell fetid corpses, so do you sense battles from afar and rush to them eagerly.'

After this terrible indictment Urban offered the knights the true way of repentance: 'If, forsooth,' he continued persuasively, 'you wish to be mindful of your souls, either lay down the girdle of such knighthood, or advance boldly, as knights of Christ, and rush as quickly as you can to the defence of the Eastern Church. For she it is from whom the joys of your whole salvation have come forth, who poured into your mouths the milk of divine wisdom, who set before you the holy teachings of the Gospels. We say this, brethren, that you may restrain your murderous hands from the destruction of your brothers, and in behalf of your relatives in the faith oppose yourselves to the Gentiles. Under Jesus Christ, our Leader, may you struggle for your Jerusalem, in Christian battleline, most invincible line . . . struggle that you may assail and drive out the Turks, more execrable than the Jebusites, who are in this land, and may you deem it a beautiful thing to die for Christ in that city in which He died for us.'

The choice was put to the western knights: the eternal damnation so richly earned by robbers and murderers; or a work for Christ equal to any undertaken by the famous Maccabees of old, for as the mystical Guibert de Nogent made it clear in his report of Urban's speech, knighthood would be granted the signal honour of seeing Christ's purpose worked out through the puny agency of miserable, sinful fighting-men: 'Consider, therefore, that the Almighty has provided you, perhaps, for this purpose, that through you He may restore Jerusalem from such debasement. Ponder, I beg you, how full of joy and delight our hearts will be when we shall see the Holy City restored with your little help, and the words of the prophet, nay the words of God, fulfilled in our times.'

In the tormented land of the Franks the invitation to a Holy War was welcomed as a release from present horrors. Weighed down by civil war and famine, France now suffered (the chronicler Ekkehard wrote) a new desolation caused by an epidemic of 'St Anthony's fire', a disease that ravaged the limbs and caused an agony leading to the maiming or death of the victim. How sweet it was to leave behind all that misery and go to practise the stirring arts of war with the blessing of the Church, to set out assured of a great adventure with the extra promise of unusual plunder. With bright and excessive hopes, hastily quitting the castle with its musty smell of old injustices, the Frankish knights rode out (though many still burdened with the impedimenta of wives, children and household goods), and braving the sneers of the Emperor's hostile lands took the sign of the cross which was to become the famous mark of the crusader. 'Oh, how fitting and pleasing to us all to see those crosses,' exclaimed Fulcher of Chartres, 'beautiful, whether of silk or woven gold or any kind of cloth, which these pilgrims, by order of Pope Urban, sewed on the shoulders of their mantles, cassocks, or tunics, once they had vowed to go.' Seeing that gallant sight of fighting-men resplendent in the tunics of the Lord, Fulcher could not withhold his praise: 'So Urban, a man prudent and revered, conceived a work whereby the whole universe later prospered.'

To Christianize the knight: all successful religions accommodate old ritual, re-edify old myth, and consecrate old sources of power. Urban's great stroke of religious policy was neither the first nor last act in a long process. Among the pagan Germans of whom Tacitus had spoken, a delivery of arms initiated the young man into the free society of warriors. Between the ritual of Teutonic tribes and the ritual of chivalry, the steps were many, obscure, but always continuous.

A youth, little more than a boy in years, stood before an older knight. He was handed the sword, the mark of his office, then the weapon in its sheath was 'girded' about his waist. The old texts speak of a blow—the *colée*—given on cheek or neck, as a test of strength or a reminder of an oath taken. This was the 'dubbing', derived from a German word meaning to strike, and this (wrote a later theorist) was the only blow a knight must accept and never return. 'He raised his hand', says the old epic *Ogier the Dane*, relating

Ogier the Dane, a famous figure from the epic poetry of the first feudal age. Carving of the 12th Cent.

The lust for battle: feudal knights in the incessant struggles of their kind. Catalan fresco of the early 13th Cent.

*Right*. The death of Roland. This illustration, from the 14th Cent *Grandes Chroniques de France*, gives the fanciful forms of late chivalry to the persons, arms and armour of this brutal early occasion.

*Opposite, top*. Charlemagne and his army march for Spain. (*Bottom*) The veteran troops return to Aachen. From a 12th Cent manuscript.

the initiation of Louis by his father Charlemagne, 'and struck his neck: "Be a knight, fair son," said the father, "and show courage in the face of the enemy."' That ceremony, typical survival of the German ritual, took place at Ratisbon in 791; and Louis in his turn, in 838, gave arms and manhood and the promise of his disordered empire to his own son Charles.

At first the ceremony was personal and general, a secular ritual confirming majority and granting freedom to take part in the adult life of the tribe. In time it became a restrictive ceremony, an initiation into the feudal order of *chevaliers*, a quite small group of armed horsemen who had certain privileges and certain duties. And being an order within the body of Christendom, the chevaliers, at a time when all of life was shot through with religious form and imagination, accepted, perhaps even solicited, the blessing of the Church on their customs. As fields and crops and herds were blessed, as house and board and marriage-bed were blessed, as all growth and fruition were blessed, as professions had a blessing on the tools of their trade, so also, in time, the dividing sword was sanctified. The weapon for the newly admitted knight was laid on the altar, and appropriate prayers composed. By the middle of the tenth century this simple liturgy was in use from London to Rome, from Germany to Spain. Later, the simple consecration of the sword was thought insufficient; it is the nature of ceremony to become complicated, more solemn, awesome. Pope Sergius, in 846, had girded Louis II with the baldric. The priest, who had once merely consecrated the sword, was soon officiating at the whole ceremony of the dubbing.

Abstinence, confession, communion purified the new knight in body and soul, consecration sanctified his deadly implements— sword, lance, shield and banner were all blessed, and only the spurs were expressly set aside as a secular gift, to be placed on the knight without the intervention of the priest. On the evening before the ceremony the Church accepted the new candidate. He was ritually bathed and then passed the night in prayer and contemplation, alone in the church. The light of day revealed the preparation of the altar, the smoke of candles and incense in the chill morning air, the wink of the sanctuary lamp, the rich cloth of vestments laid out for bishop and priest and numerous acolytes. The candidate, his confession made, advanced before the congregation of well-wishers and came to the Mass.

After the Gradual of the Mass came the ritual of knighthood, a ceremony described in its full flowering by the thirteenth-century *Pontifical* of Bishop Guillaume Durand of Mende. Taking up the bare sword, the Bishop laid it on the altar with these words: 'Bless this sword, that Thy servant may henceforth defence churches, widows, orphans, and all those who serve God, against the cruelty of heretics and infidels. Bless this sword Holy Lord, Almighty Father, Eternal God. Bless it in the name of the coming of Christ and by the gift of the Holy Ghost the Comforter. And may Thy servant, armed with Thy love, tread all his visible enemies underfoot, and, master of victory, rest forever protected from all attack.' The prayer

*Left.* The investiture of the knight with the arms of his calling. 12th Cent carving from the cloisters at Elne.

The girding of the sword on the young knight. From a Flemish manuscript, 1280.

Knights on campaign: the scene in camp. Spanish fresco from the reign of Jaime I.

Portrait of knights, an illustration from a treatise on warfare, dated 1028. Apart from the pennant on the lance, these early mounted warriors display none of the later heraldic and colourful trappings of chivalry. A grim and shaggy appearance testifies to their uncouth ways, so too does the baleful expression of the horses' eyes.

40

Fighting knights. Wall-painting of
the 13th Cent from Tour Ferrande,
Pernes, France.

Sir Galahad receives sword and spurs in the solemn Church ritual of knighthood. From a manuscript of *Tristan* dated 1463.

of the righteous soldier is read from the Old Testament: 'Blessed be the Lord God who formeth my hands for battle and my fingers for war. He is my salvation, He is my refuge, He setteth me free'; and then, in the name of the Trinity, the Bishop places the sword in the right hand of the knight, receives it back, delivers the *colée*, and girds the weapon about the waist of the kneeling warrior. In gratitude and affirmation of his new power, the knight brandishes the sword three times and returns it to the scabbard; he is now 'marked with the character of knighthood'. The Bishop advances again with the final kiss of peace and an admonition to Christian virtue: 'Be a soldier peaceful, courageous, faithful, and devoted to God.'

Such was the ritual of dubbing according to the grandest ceremonial, refined in the leisurely days of peace. In practice, neither in peace nor in war were the clergy indispensable. In war, men were of necessity dubbed on the field, the quick touch of the sword on the shoulder giving the *colée*, the accolade, which was by itself sufficient to confer knighthood. In peace, the dubbing was often performed, still with great solemnity but without benefit of clergy. In the romance *Galeran* the dubbing becomes a secular festivity, hung with blues and golds, adorned with the emblem of the double eagle. The Duke of Lorraine puts the right spur on the hero Galeran, and gives him a damascened sword with golden pommel; the Duchess hangs the shield round his neck. The dubbing itself is an honour undertaken by an elder knight who girds Galeran with the sword and gives him the ritual blow with the right hand. The day is given up to feasting, and the next day to tournament, the new knights riding out in full armour through the banner-hung town, to the sound of music and the continual pealing of bells. But even in the midst of his secular joy, the religious signification of knighthood is not forgotten. After the blow of the accolade, the knight who has given it addresses Galeran: 'Knight, may God move you to high honour in all things and make you a *prudhomme* in thought, word, and deed.' And then the company go into Mass, the new knights receiving communion in their armour.

By the time of the First Crusade men said commonly that a knight was 'ordained'. A pagan ceremony which had merely confirmed the majority of the tribal warrior had been transformed, through the intervention of the Church, into a ritual which some did not hesitate to call a 'sacrament'. The Church had cast her supernatural spell on the feudal knights, the most potent force in society, and had attempted to bind them, through initiation, to the active service of the faith. Ecclesiastical writers considered that all knights were bound by obligations which were stated in the oath that the new knight swore at the altar during the ceremony of the dubbing. Even those dubbed outside the Church were said to agree tacitly, by reason of knighthood itself, to the general obligation. And one of the terms of the oath was inevitably the practice and defence of the true faith.

The words were easily said and forgotten, for no knight thought of himself as anything but an orthodox Christian and a dutiful son of the Church. The abasement of the new knight before the altar, an act that in theory so fatefully subdued the knight to the moral law, in practice, by itself, quite failed to correct the customary evil of old feudal habits. Elevated sentiments made little impression on rough understandings thoroughly at home in the old quarrelsome ways. Then Pope Urban flung out the challenge of Jerusalem lost, summoned a Crusade, and revealed a task for Christian knighthood. A conscious idealism was born. The knight, thinking of himself with amazement as the true Christian bulwark against the infidel, began to see himself in the light of half-forgotten oaths and take seriously old obligations.

'All your blood', said the *Ordène de Chevalerie*, 'you must shed in defence of Holy Church.' And this admonition was taken seriously by the new chivalric warrior. The high ideal is best expressed in the rules that the great enthusiast Ramon Lull drew up in his *Book of the Order of Chivalry*. 'The office of knight', declared this rigorist, 'is to maintain and defend the holy faith catholic . . . and to honour and multiply the faith which has suffered in this world many travails, despites, and anguished death.' We see in literature and history a recognition of the rightness of this rule, and the struggle of knights to live according to this high sentence.

The rule of chaos in the 10th Cent:
an early stone castle stands on its
mound behind a palisade, resisting
the attackers who use battering-
rams and crossbows. From a
manuscript, *c*. 1009.

*Right*. The Church welcomes and
comforts the pilgrims. From an
illustrated psalter of the 13th Cent.

'Do not forget, you knights,' says the Archbishop of Rheims at the beginning of *Garin li Loherains*, 'that God has called you to be the rampart of the Church.' This responsibility was sometimes accepted, very often neglected, but hardly ever denied. Even the most barbarous of the epic heroes gave a religious colouring to their very crimes. 'My son,' the mother of Raoul de Cambrai entreats him, 'never destroy either church or chapel, and for God's sake, never make the poor homeless.' Raoul, whose ferocious anger did all that his mother feared and more besides, perversely made the very destruction he caused a consequence of a holy oath, such was the force of chivalric habit: 'Raoul's head was bowed on his hand, and he swore by God who was born of a Virgin that for all the gold of Toledo he would not give up his fief until many an entrail had been strewn and many a brain scattered.' Rank atheists are few in the literature. There is one who prays to the devil in the shambles of a foundering ship, makes the sign of the cross backwards and sinks defiantly beneath the waves; there is another theatrical fellow who advises service neither to God nor truth: 'If you meet an honest man,' he says, 'dishonour him. Burn down towns, villages and houses; overthrow the altars and break the crucifixes.' But the writers display the great majority of heroes as men driven to habitual violence by overmastering passion, though well aware of a knight's religious duty. They die like Raoul de Cambrai, in a black fury but calling on Christ and his Mother: 'May God receive his soul', the poet concluded, 'if we dare pray on his behalf!'

The poets of the old epic knew very well the troubled mind of knighthood, brutal self-interest contending with the new Christian chivalry. 'This Saracen appears a great heretic,' Archbishop Turpin mutters to himself in the *Chanson de Roland*; 'The best course is for me to go and slay him.' And so he does, taking the sword to the infidel as the Church enjoined. But the responsibility of the faith was a hard one, which a knight would acknowledge but avoid if he could, usually preferring to fight for the sake of his disreputable ambition. At the end of *Roland*, Charlemagne is summoned by the angel Gabriel to gather his armies once more and lead them against the pagans, for the Christians 'cry aloud and call on you'. The old Emperor, the paladin of the faith, is obstinate, weeping complaints and tugging at his white beard in despair. 'God,' he groans, 'how wearisome is my life.'

How well the historical knight, following the path of chivalry against the infidel, came to know the weariness of the great King. In Syrian dust, by some stinking water-hole in Palestine, enclosed in burning armour under an Egyptian sun, how he wished to be rid of his high office and engaged once more in the pleasant banditry of his verdant homeland. Yet constant backslider that he was, something made him acknowledge the force of the ideal he followed so lamely, whether he expressed it in the blunt words of St Louis, that 'a layman, as soon as he hears the Christian faith maligned, should defend it only by the sword, with a good thrust in the belly, as far as the sword will go', or whether he echoed the more elegant admonition of the lord of Bourlemont to his cousin Joinville: 'You

assumed the sign of the cross to hurry thither, unless they are prevented by the hindrance of poverty'. The sword was reforged into the true servant of the Church. In the *Pontifical* of Guillaume Durand, the new knight prayed to God 'who hast permitted on earth the use of the sword to repress the malice of the wicked and to defend justice; who for the protection of Thy people hast thought fit to institute the order of chivalry'.

Soon after Urban's call, in the flush of enthusiasm, triumphant with sanctity, the sword entered into more formal liaison with religion. Before the coming of the Seljuq Turks there was established in Jerusalem a benevolent order of men and women devoted to the care of western pilgrims: these were the Hospitallers, bound by monastic vows, useful if sombre figures under black gowns with the eight-pointed star on the breast, symbolic of the Beatitudes. Suspended by Turkish rule, the order rose in new glory after 1099, plentifully endowed (Godfrey of Bouillon gave the income from his Brabant estates), and soon added offensive weapons to their more usual implements of medicine and care. Around 1118 the males of the order were reconstituted into the Brethren of St John of Jerusalem, a fighting order, still under monastic vows, committed to the defence of the kingdom of Jerusalem, but still undertaking also charitable care of pilgrims.

The precedent set by the Hospitallers, of men under vow and under arms, was soon followed wherever infidel or pagan threatened Christian lands. The Teutonic Knights, formed about 1128 and restricted to Germans, were at first associated with the Hospitallers, but distinguished from them by white cloak and black cross. After the loss of the Holy Land they established themselves at Marienburg in Prussia, grim guardians of a desolate north. In Spain and Portugal the military orders of Avis, Compostella, Calatrava, and Alcantara fought to drive the Moors from the peninsula.

*Left*. St Denis giving a standard to the Crusader Clement de Metz. From a 13th Cent window in Chartres Cathedral.

A knight makes a disposition of his property before taking up the Crusading call of the Church. From a 13th Cent manuscript.

The worn figures on this Templar seal reflect something of the austere purpose of the first Knight of the Temple.

Hospitallers and Teutonic Knights combined fighting with the care of sick and poor. The famous Knights of the Temple, first coming together by the Temple in Jerusalem and formally constituted in 1128, were altogether fiercer, living only for the defence of the Holy Places and the protection of pilgrims. Such an aggressive intention in monastic form was religion in strange dress; later ages found the Templars a dangerous power, full of pride, greed and heresy; the order was suppressed with the greatest cruelty. But the sense of holy gallantry in the first chivalric soldiers induced even St Bernard, a man who had seen and rejected ordinary knighthood, to give his authority to the rule of the Templars. The Saint who had once condemned the 'gigantic error', the 'intolerable madness' of knights who 'fight with such expense and labour for no reward, save that of death' found sufficient reason for the blood and death caused by 'the poor Soldiers of Jesus Christ'.

In the white robe, emblem of purity, adorned with the red cross, emblem of blood, was not a Templar the very antithesis of the self-seeking feudal knight? The latter was wedded to luxury, ambition, riches; the former to bare subsistence, obedience, poverty. The latter studied fashion idly, hunted from his gilded saddle, feasted to lascivious music; the former hardly rested from holy service, driving on in relentless disarray, 'never brushed, seldom washed, hair shaggy and tangled, besmirched with dust, with dull armour, burnt up by the sun'. The quarrels of the latter were the shame of society; the wars of the former were the painful duty of the just.

St Bernard, from a window in Le Mans Cathedral.

'They can fight the battles of the Lord and can be certain that they are the soldiers of Christ,' said Bernard in his *De laudibus novae militiae*, a justification of the Templars written for the Grand Master:

> Let them kill the enemy or die; they need have no fear. To embrace death for Christ or to cause His enemies to submit to it is nothing but glory: it is no crime. Moreover it is not without reason that the soldier of Christ carries a sword. It is for the chastisement of the wicked and for the glory of the good. If it bring death to the malefactor, the soldier is not a homicide but (excuse the word) a "malicide". And we must recognize in him the avenger who is in the service of Christ, and the liberator of the Christian people.

The approval of Bernard, a saint hardly less persuasive in his time than Augustine himself, set a crown on the new military chivalry. 'The highest order that God has made and willed', said the rhapsodist Chrétien de Troyes, 'is the order of chivalry.' Few knights, indeed, followed the new military precepts with any strictness; the twelfth century, which saw the growth and elaboration of the code of chivalry, saw also some of the most brutal warfare of the Middle Ages, and not least among the crusaders. But the few who did follow the Christian precepts of war exemplified an heroic ideal of manly conduct which stood out so starkly from the mire of selfish action, that the gallant chevaliers impressed quite out of proportion to their small numbers. Such knights as Godfrey of Bouillon were

*Opposite.* Memorial to Count Hughes de Vaudémont and his wife, from the Church of the Cordeliers at Nancy. Count Hughes, whose arduous Crusading history was so typical of his age, returned after sixteen years in the Holy Land, in which time his family had given him up for dead.

Godfrey of Bouillon, a leader of the First Crusade and the first King of Jerusalem, on the journey to the Holy Land. From a 14 Cent manuscript.

not without admirers even among the Arabs. And Usama ibn Munqidh, a political realist who spent most of his long life intimately among the crusaders, has testified to the tact, courtesy and devotion of the early Templars.

If the enemy was respectful, how much more so were the theorists within Christendom. Mainly churchmen (for learning and exposition were chiefly in the hands of the Church), these men set out the virtues of the new chivalry with a sense of surprised congratulation at the fine garment the Church had wrought out of the rank material of feudal knighthood. Wishfully, they acclaimed a new, disinterested force in society, bound by religious oath to the moral law, an adjunct to good government, able to compensate for the weakness of kings, or to withstand the tyranny of vassals. 'Cause they servant here before thee', ran the noble prayer of the knightly initiate in the *Pontifical*, 'by disposing his heart to goodness, never to use this sword or another to injure anyone unjustly; but let him use it always to defend the just and the right.' The body of men illuminated by such generosity, hardy, watchful, disciplined, was (said John of Salisbury) 'the armed hand of the state'. Knights are properly chosen 'rather for their faith and morals than for their strength', wrote Vincent of Beauvais, and the purpose of these

knights is 'to protect the Church, to attack disloyalty, to reverence priests, to avenge the wrongs of the poor, and to keep the country in a state of quiet'.

For a moment, at its birth, under the democratic influence of Christian idealism, chivalry seemed to deny the aristocratic social privilege claimed by feudal knighthood, and soon to be reclaimed by the profane courtly chivalry of a later age. In the view of the Church, chivalry was open to all good men of sound body. In theory, any knight could confer knighthood, and a villein was as eligible as a noble. Some held that a soldier might knight himself in the desperation of battle, as Archbishop Turpin did in the tale of *Aspremont*. And surely many a low-born man was knighted. The old poets, faithful witnesses to the spirit of the age, portray such base-born fellows as Varocher, the scowling wood-cutter who protects the Queen of France and her son from the dangers of exile and persecution and is knighted by the Emperor for his loyalty. The historical complaint of later knights in Germany, anxious to repair the breach in the barrier of class distinction, that too many merchants, craftsmen and other undesirables were being admitted to their confraternity, proved the widespread occurrence of knights raised from low estate.

A short moment of equality, then pride of class re-established itself, and thoroughly secular appetites moved chivalry away from the religious idealism that first nourished it. Chivalry was fostered by the Church, but the men who professed it were not part of the Church; they were, at heart, the same turbulent dogs who had set Europe on fire in the tenth century, and they found austerity, humility, piety hard words to stomach. Chivalry never forgot the symbolism, the ardour, the sense of mystery that religion taught it. But the plainer lesson of painful endeavour and high religious and moral purpose that Urban had preached, that Godfrey of Bouillon had practised, and that St Bernard had approved, was generally neglected. Ancestral pride, profane desires, twisted the simplicity of the first chivalry into arcane, luxurious strands.

# chapter three

After the early elation, and the first hope of escape from persistent troubles, what was the common expectation of the crusading knight? Apprehension at parting, fear and pain and loneliness in absence, failure in battle, grief and disillusion in recollection.

'What sighs, what weepings,' wrote the chronicler Fulcher of a scene enacted so many times, 'what lamentations among friends, when the husband left his dear wife, and his children, and all his possessions, his father, his mother, his brothers, his relatives.' The tearful wife 'was unable to stand and fell senseless to the ground and wept for her love, whom, though still living, she gave up for dead already'. And the departing knight, all stubborn stoicism, 'like one who had no pity (though he had), and as if moved neither by the tears of his wife nor by the grief of his friends (yet in his heart he was moved), set out, keeping his purpose firm'.

The time away seemed an exile. The memory of distant home, and the stronger thought of uncertainties and dangers that might surround it, made the suffering of the campaign harder to endure. William of Poitiers, the man accounted the first troubadour, having taken the cross of the Crusader in 1101, sang for all those who felt the bitterness of the separation. He grieved for his dear young son, left in the care of a rival lord; he grieved for the fate of his own 'fair Poitou', in the hands of that same dangerous lord. He who was once so 'gracious and gay' now felt the burden of crusading responsibility. All his former delight—his happiness, his pride, his knighthood, his possessions—he offered up to God for the remission of his sins and the consequent relief from fear and misery.

The practice of military chivalry was an incessant toil. 'I have

Young knights at archery practice.
*Romance of Alexander, c.* 1340.

ridden with you through all Greece,' the troubadour Raembaut de Vaqueiras wrote to the lord of Montferrat, 'have given and taken many a hard blow, have fallen and made others fall, have fled and pursued with you, have fought on water and on bridges, have broken through steady ranks, and taken prisoners with you, kings and princes.' Many delighted in this knight-errantry, finding it the way to reputation and adventure. 'Something of war let there be left to me, when naught but peace I see around,' cried the ever-riotous Bertran de Born; 'Peace small joy doth give, one with strife I'll live.' 'Roland and Oliver in one am I,' boasted the vainglorious Peire Vidal. But many men, in the pride of knighthood, yet of a peaceful inclination, or bred in quieter places, regretted the waste and pain of continual fighting.

What made a journey to a far dry land indispensable for the practice of chivalry? The hope of chivalry was not just to make armed ascetics on the model of the Templars, but to civilize the powerful and dangerous warriors of the west, and any code for their improvement must take account, not just of war, but of all their activities. There was a part of the new ideal that had to do with the courtesy, elegance and attainments judged necessary for the leaders of society. And there was a part that had to do with worldly pleasures and the delights of peace.

In our gentle western climate, far from the desert heat where the raw bones of the earth wore through the thin skin of dust, the turn of the seasons insinuated its potent magic. 'Winter's untruth', as a wandering poet memorably called it, yielded to the return of spring. Disreputable Goliard poets, pleasure-loving itinerant scholars in hostage to the varying fortune of their erratic lives, celebrated

Preliminary training in the use of the lance, on foot, in the tiltyard. *Romance of Alexander, c.* 1340.

the universal joy of men in unsettled times, dismissing the anxiety of the dark and fervently greeting the end of winter oppression. Pain, all sad thoughts and passions fly at the advent of spring. Sun, fruition, increase inspired thoughts of pleasure. For many knights who answered the call in an ignorant enthusiasm, a crusade was penance, a kind of winter of the spirit, to be banished by a vigorous reflux of

Daily life: the middle band of this tympanum presents a hunting scene; the lowest band gives the typical tasks of the countryside according to the months of the year. A 12th Cent carving from Bourges.

sap in the veins in the springtime of their return. The religious austerity of military chivalry was often replaced by a scandalous excess of pagan vitality.

William of Poitiers, troubadour and reluctant crusader, set the shocking example. This 'giddy, unsettled kind of man' (wrote William of Malmesbury), after his return from Jerusalem, 'wallowed as completely in the sty of vice as though he believed that all things were governed by chance and not by Providence. . . . Finally he erected near a castle called Niort, certain buildings after the form of a little monastery, and used to talk idly about placing therein an abbey of whores, naming several of the most abandoned courtesans, one as abbess, another as prioress. Repudiating his lawful consort, he carried off the wife of a certain count, of whom he was so desperately enamoured, that he placed on his shield the figure of this woman; affirming that he was as desirous of bearing her in battle in the same manner as she bore him at another time.'

The absurdities and humours of William of Poitiers were, his pious chronicler had to admit, enlivened 'by a kind of satirical wit which excited the great amusement of his hearers'. The chronicler had detected the nascent spirit of a secular, courtly chivalry, in which the exercise of wit and imagination mattered as much as the exercise of arms, which acknowledged the ideals of Christian mili-

57

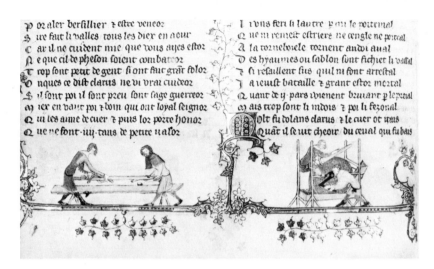

*Top.* Care and preparation of weapons. *Bottom.* Training with the crossbow. *Romance of Alexander,* c. 1340.

tary chivalry, sometimes respectfully, sometimes in parody, was often indecent, occasionally blasphemous.

In 1095, seeking ready ground on which to cultivate the new strain of chivalrous idealism, Pope Urban came to Auvergne, in the south, in the country of the Languedoc. And in this soil his words took hold and prospered. The first of the great men of the west to take up the papal call was Raymond of Saint-Gilles, Count of Toulouse, the one-eyed visionary who, in wealth and power, was hardly inferior to the King of France. He led and the knights of the southland followed, from Provence, Toulouse, Gascony and Aquitaine, from the still Mediterranean to the raw Atlantic, from the Pyrenees almost to the banks of the Loire, brothers in a greater prosperity and a greater ease than the cold north enjoyed, and united in the tongue of Languedoc, the ancient Provençal language.

This land was favoured by geography, by history, by a continuous conflux of races. The unwavering Mediterranean sun made the fields fruitful: vineyards and olive-groves of unrecoverable antiquity, wheat, almonds, fruits of many kinds, in particular citrus fruits and figs, mulberries, chestnuts. Good produce brought traders, and traders settlement and civilization. Roman traditions and institutions still lived, cities founded by Greeks or Romans—Marseilles, Arles, Nîmes, Toulouse—still thrived. Many centuries of trade had allowed an accumulation of wealth and guaranteed a present prosperity. Civic institutions were well advanced. Warfare was known, against the Moors across the Pyrenees, and between the petty fiefdoms of the land; but the more severe and enervating strife of the Holy Roman Empire, which pulled down so much of continental Europe, passed by; the lands of Languedoc were beyond the ambition of the Emperor, and the local princes were too strong for him. Indeed, the Count of Provence, the Count of Toulouse, and the Duke of Aquitaine were independent powers who did not fear kings.

The training of the knight: young men exercise, wrestle, and practise their weapons while an artist paints a statue. From a 13th Cent translation of Cicero's *Rhetoric*.

In the early twelfth century the famous Raymond Berangar, Count of Barcelona, beat the Moors out of Aragon, incorporated Aragon and Barcelona with Provence, and formed a little empire over which his troubadour son, Alfonso II, reigned in some magnificence. The country of Toulouse, ruled by a succession of Raymonds famous (or notorious) for their crusading exploits, kept its strength until destroyed by the Albigensian War. In Aquitaine, the witty and irreverent William of Poitiers held luxurious court in Bordeaux. His grand-daughter Eleanor was a catch worthy of two kings, marrying first the French and then the English monarch. She brought Aquitaine as dowry to her English husband, Henry II, and her son, Richard Lionheart, became later Duke of Aquitaine, a promoter of feudal struggle and the friend of troubadours.

Phoenicians had been in the land; Greeks, Romans, Byzantines and Arabs had followed. The mark of many exemplary cultures was on the people. Warfare, the preoccupation of northern nobles so threatened by invaders, was not the same worry in the south. The great princes kept stately courts, friendly to arts and learning. But the smaller nobles, in the twelfth century, also kept wit alive in Roussillon, Foix, Béarn, Limousin, Périgord, Auvergne and many other small local courts. There was the example of the great: was not Count William of Poitiers reckoned the first troubadour? And did not such

Education and entertainment of the knight: a medieval war game, from the *Hortus deliciarum* of Herrade de Landsbourg.

mighty nobles as Alfonso and Richard Lionheart follow in the exacting discipline of poetry? But men of fewer resources also supported art with an almost ruinous generosity. The twelfth-century *Lives of the Troubadours* relates of Robert of Auvergne that 'there was no knight in all the world so wise and courteous, so bountiful and warlike as he, and none so versed in love, and gallantry, and deeds of chivalry, and none his like in learning and understanding'. This prodigal

The training of the knight: arms practice with sword, lance and crossbow. From *Secreta fidelium crucis*, 1321.

noble reduced his lands to a half 'by his bountiful gifts', but he expected, the writer of the *Lives* suggested, the more enduring reward of a duty done to the spirit of men, 'and thereafter to win unto himself all that he had lost, yea, and much more besides'. Pope Urban was not wrong to begin the search for idealism in the territory of Auvergne.

Strange airs blew from the Mediterranean, airs carrying an influence emanating from Greece, from Asia Minor, from Arabia, from North Africa. The life of Languedoc was feudal, but tempered by memories both ancient and alien. Sunlight, propitious airs, abundant wine, discourse and speculation that were just as intoxicating, more leisure, all gave a touch of unfamiliar splendour to the south. Feudal division seemed less harsh than elsewhere. The southern peasant was likely to be in easier circumstances than his northern counterpart, more knowledgeable, less servile. The merchants of the long-established towns had already won a standing in the land, the importance of their commerce being apparent even to the rural feudal nobility, who affected to despise trade. Men were more gathered into towns than elsewhere, and felt the civilized benefits that town life can bring. Intellectual ferment was capable of breaking down feudal barriers, forming a kind of democracy of letters. The troubadour Bernart de Ventadorn, said the *Lives*, 'was one of low degree, to wit son of a serving-man, who gathered brushwood for the oven where the castle bread was baked'. He was made the intimate of his lord and 'became a fair man and skilled, and knew well to make poetry and to sing, and was both courteous and learned'. Giraut de Borneil, named the Master of Troubadors, was also of villein birth. Peire d'Auvergne, Folquet, Gaucelm Faidit, all notable

Itinerant jongleur of the Languedoc playing on an instrument, probably the shawm, the ancestor of the modern oboe. From an 11th Cent manuscript from the south-west of France.

poets, were sons of townsmen; the father of the impetuous Peire Vidal was a furrier; all were raised to a higher estate, consorted with lords, aspired to noble women.

The feudal lord, to whom rectitude came from the practice of simple military virtues, felt the insistent flow of ancient speculation, insinuating into his rough scheme of life not only the Christian voices of the great church-fathers, but also the troubled experience of the pagan Plato, the Jew Maimonides, the Moslem Avicenna. That was the peculiarity of the south: the violent warrior life of brigandage and pride and honour subtly encompassed and softened by refining influences. An acquaintance with many kinds of thought, some wealth, more leisure, made a land receptive to, even eager for, an ideal of a new life. There was a degree of experiment, a departure from convention, in the south which seemed highly suspicious to the traditional-minded men of the north. As usual, critics saw daring in fashion as the beginning of decadence. Ordericus Vitalis dated the corruption of morals from the years just before the First Crusade, and found the decay spread as far as the Loire, to the court of Fulk Nerra: 'Now worldly men dress proudly in accordance with their perverse habits. What was formerly a disgrace to an honourable man, those of this age find as sweet as honey, and parade as a special distinction. The customs of the barbarian have been adopted in their dress and in their lives. They have parted their hair down the middle of the head, and grown long locks like women, and put on long shirts and tunics, tied tight with points. Now most people have their hair and beards curled, bearing on their faces the emblem of their filthy lusts, like stinking goats.' Dangerous movements were afoot, inflamed by poetry.

In unlettered ages the poet is the custodian of the past. Every early society needs its Homer, for he is the living record of tradition and the teacher of manners. The part the minstrel played in the making of western society is a topic obscured by a disapproving Church, for official history was largely in the hands of churchmen who were keen to deny poetry its proper place in the story. Songs and epics handed down by mouth have generally disappeared, and the unnamed singers themselves make only a fleeting appearance through the hostile reticence of the church chroniclers. One divines their ghostly but continuous presence through outbursts and interjections, the rancorous footnotes to the official page. In England, we learn that one of the early acts of Christianity, in 679, prohibited the clergy from keeping *citharoedae*, who were most probably the native English minstrels. Sixty years later a council had to remind the English hierarchy that monasteries were not fit places for poets, players, singers, jugglers, clowns and the like.

The very opposition of the Church indicated the strong hold of the English 'scop' and 'gleeman', and of the Norman 'jongleur' who followed them. Churchmen themselves dared the wrath of the Church, so infatuated were they with song and recitation. An abbot of Newcastle sent surreptitiously to a foreign bishop asking for a *citharoeda*. Most scandalously, a priest in the diocese of Worcester forgets himself at the altar and chants 'Sweet lemman, thine ore' instead of 'Dominus vobiscum'. Kings and princes have no need to hide their love of minstrels. It is acknowledged that the minstrel's place is by the great man's side, and an authentic tradition recorded in poetry has it that the minstrel alone can travel safely through the war-torn land. One story recalls King Alfred visiting the Danish camp in the guise of a minstrel. And Olaf, the Viking King, penetrates the camp of Athelstan at Brunanburg in a similar disguise. The story is so pervasive it is repeated impartially, sometimes as history, sometimes as legend. The *History of Britain* by Geoffrey of Monmouth has Balduf crossing the enemy lines in the dress of a minstrel to reach his brother in York. In the tale of *King Horn*, the hero impersonates a harper to gain admission to the castle. War and peace were equally provinces of the minstrel. William of Malmesbury spoke of a '*cantilena Rolandi*' chanted at the battle of Hastings, and the poet Wace expanded this hint into the well-known episode of the jongleur Taillefer riding before Duke William into battle, tossing his sword into the air and singing 'of Charlemagne and of Roland and of Oliver and of the vassals who died at Roncesvalles'. Was it not

A courtly greeting: trumpeters perform from the castle walls, the ladies look on, while minstrels with rebec and lyre accompany the scene. Detail from a Sicilian bedspread.

the proper task of the minstrel to remind the army of ancestral heroes, and incite the warriors to similar deeds?

A world was passing, one of continuous struggle, invasion, sudden death, an epic world commemorated by the poets of the Nordic sagas, of *Beowulf*, of *Roland* and the other *chansons de geste*. At the millennium, in the time of settlement, a new world advanced, ushered in by poetry, fashioned perhaps as much by poetry and language as by any other factor. This has been called the world of romance. The unavoidable obligations of the first feudal age, to repel the invader or to die, made no quality or emotion more important than those of the fighting-man: the epic poet sang of courage, strength, endurance, loyalty; he did not concern himself with love, beauty, delicacy, learning. The drawing back from the edge of an

appalling doom made power less important, and other themes came to be treated, themes perhaps less noble than the simplicities of raw life and a hard death, but also more intricate, more subtle and problematic. Did the epic poet recognize the vanishing inspiration and the need for change? One of the last seemed to imply it. Celebrating the Viking raid of Olaf Tryggvason, and the battle against him at Maldon, on the Essex coast, in 993, the poet wrote: 'Thought shall be harder, heart the keener, mood the more, as our might lessens.'

Images of blood cleared from the sight. Appetites, vigour and joy once subdued by the necessity for struggle and the fear of death were re-expressed with new force in new words. The return of the light was greeted again by the *alba*, the dawn-song: 'Slumber no more, shake off the dreams of night, from the east the speeding star brings in its train the light of day.' That dawn caused a great awakening from the night of feudal violence. Enlightenment touched first the lands of Languedoc. The celebrated voices of Provençal poetry announced the new day.

The circumstances leading to that sudden illumination are profoundly mysterious. The moment rested on complexities of culture, complexities of inheritance, on an oral tradition formed by the words of the poet in the mouth of the singer. The moment may be placed between 1095 and 1100, between Urban's speech at Clermont and the first known poem of the first known troubadour; the true antecedents of that moment may only be guessed at. It drew on the lyric possibilities of medieval Latin demonstrated equally by the hymns of the Church and by the licentious, not to say pagan, chants of the wandering Goliard scholars, lyric possibilities gradually transmuted from Latin into its derivative Provençal, the first modern Romance language to reach full development and the tongue in which modern poetry began. It drew also on music, on the necessity of the new lyric to be sung and on the profound desire of an audience to hear the melodies.

Homer, that ancient professional minstrel, declared in the *Odyssey* that the gods weave sorrows into the loom of events so that the poet may sing of them for future generations. The gods had decreed an end to the epic pattern composed of suffering, and instituted a lyric pattern in which the strands were joy and hope, love and pleasure. The troubadours perceived the new strain, and Provençal was the medium for their song. They were heard by the knighthood of the west, at first by the nobles of southern France, but soon throughout all Christendom. In that age men learnt by the spoken word, not by the written page. Chance winds took the jongleur, the minstrel, freely through all Europe and his songs went with him. Differences of language were no constraint. Minds trained by the necessity to remember, rather than to read, handled language far more easily than later book-bound, more self-conscious ages. All educated people in the west had behind them the common language of Latin, the common faith of Christendom, and a common culture based on Roman and Christian sources. Martin Luther used to say that a Fleming tied in a sack and carried from Flanders to Italy would learn the languages of the countries he passed through on the way. And four centuries before Luther the mental passage from land to land was easier still. Thoughts and ideals instituted and broadcast by the troubadours were soon the property of all Christendom.

The troubadour was no mere jongleur, though he might start as one if he were poor: he was, as the name implies, a 'maker', a composer of lyrics for the jongleur to perform. No doubt the rising poet from a poor family was still the jongleur for his own songs, and successful poets on occasion condescended to perform. But the established troubadour would acquire—a mark of his superiority— his own jongleur; it is said of the great poet Giraut de Borneil that, although of low birth, he went from court to court accompanied by his own two singers. These poets were no court entertainers; there were always jugglers, tumblers, mimes, singers, musicians sufficient for that purpose, content with a word of praise, a place at table, a long pull at the servants' wine-jug, and a silver coin tossed casually on the rushes of the floor. The troubadour was a valued man, an arbiter, a learned man: Giraut 'was wont to pass the winter in the schools, in the study of letters'.

Poetry was both profession and avocation. Men, and women, came to it from all parts of society, but when they were found worthy to be called troubadour they were raised to a new dignity. They were courtly figures, in friendly contention with kings, princes and nobles. Many were themselves knights, or aspired to knighthood. The qualities they admired in others, and often looked for in themselves, were knightly qualities. They found an ideal for both man and poet in such high-born troubadours as William of Poitiers, 'one of the most courteous men in the world,' said the *Lives of the Troubadours*, 'a valiant knight in warfare, and bounteous in love and gallantry'; or in Jaufre Rudel, 'the right noble prince of Blaye'; or (expressing both ideals more fully) in Robert, Count of Auvergne, 'none so versed in love and gallantry, and deeds of chivalry, and none his like in learning and understanding, and in the making of *coblas*, and *sirventes*, *sons*, and *tensons*'; or, at last, in the shining example of Pons de Capduoil, 'a noble baron of the diocese of Puy Sainte-Marie, who made poetry and sang and violed full well. And he was valiant in battle, and learned, and courteous, and chivalrous, and fair-spoken, and of great stature and comeliness.'

The first troubadours sang of the preoccupations of knights. They wrote *sirventes* on war and politics and noble rivalries, *tensons* on the disputes of courtiers; they were satirical like Marcabrun, active and angry like Bertran de Born, boastful like Peire Vidal, cutting and censorious like the Monk of Montaldon. Their enemies were the enemies of knighthood: upstart and disobedient peasants, rich townsmen threatening the sanctity of the feudal order, clergy who criticized knights yet themselves led corrupt and privileged lives. They turned into song the pride, the aggression, the independence and the prejudice of feudal knights. And the peculiarity of their genius was to give lyrical expression to these stern qualities descending from a former epic age. And they added one new element, one all-important element implicit in lyricism and implicit also in the sophistication of the south: they added the principle of pleasure to the necessities of the knightly life; they sang of ease and beauty and love.

Pope Urban had called for a life of service against the infidel. The troubadour knights had tasted that fruit and found it bitter. After the complaint of William of Poitiers against crusading, even the most quarrelsome of troubadours would do his best to avoid the pains of the Holy Land. That most likely warrior, Peire Vidal, set out for the Third Crusade in a fit of rashness induced by despairing love, but his resolve began to fail as the homeland receded, and he never advanced beyond Cyprus. Characteristic troubadour opinion agreed with the regret expressed by the early poet Marcabrun: 'Cursed be King Louis who did send, to bid all men Christ's tomb defend, whereby my breast with grief is filled.' But none the less the troubadours, children of ease and learning, were strongly stirred by the current of Urban's thought and greatly attracted to an idealized aristocratic life; but in the propaganda of their songs they substituted the ideal of courtly pleasure and sophistication for the more rigorous ideal of Christian service. In their eyes, the knight of chivalry was still a warrior, still the favoured of God, still the feudal leader of the people, but he was also a gentleman, a scholar, perhaps a poet, certainly a lover.

Was there not something magically persuasive in this fresh concept of valour blended with delicacy, and activity tempered by thought? Even in the naïve ranting of Peire Vidal, an innocent confidence and geniality win admiration. He was (he claimed) not only the equal of Roland and Oliver, but also vied with the greatest name in courtesy: 'In my lady's bower', he congratulated himself, 'none is more courteous and debonair; none, in the battlefield, is of greater power.' The ancient epic heroes have the pathetic dignity of true men going to meet a cruel destiny. But which of those mighty warriors, what Roland or Oliver, would have revelled, as Peire Vidal did, in the plentitude of human happiness, and the goodness of the earth:

> Great joy have I to greet the season bright,
> And joy to greet the blessed summer days,
> And joy when birds do carol songs of praise,
> And joy to mark the woods with flowers dight,
> And joy at all whereat to joy were meet.

The beginning of a keener sensibility did not mean an end to war. The chivalric knight was still bred to fight; warfare was the one business he thoroughly understood. And indeed the expense of an elegant court was likely to drive the baron into the field, for honour and for profit, the plunder of a campaign being reckoned a large and easy part of a noble's income. 'If I robbed,' said one of the troubadour-knights, 'it was to give, not to hoard.' The heavy wagons, in *Garin li Loherains*, follow hard on the heels of the troops, waiting for the spoils of war. The poet Bertran de Born knew very well the advantages of war; for his own well-being, as a petty fief-holder and troubadour, depended greatly on the liberality of greater nobles. 'Why do I wish rich men to hate each other?' he asked in his usual forthright way. 'Because a rich man is much more noble and generous and affable in war than in peace.' And battling nobles needed the service of energetic, unscrupulous vassals like Bertran. He became, therefore, an intrepid promoter of discord, ready to take any side for money. 'I have already a shield about my neck and a helm on my head,' he told the Count of Poitiers, 'but how can I put myself in the field without money?' Bertran, condemned by Dante to the circles of hell, owes his dubious fame to this selfish turbulence.

The necessities of warfare framed the whole life of the knight. And courtly chivalry, far from being a revulsion from fighting, was rather an exaltation of the fighting-man, giving a formal elegance and polish to the raw qualities of the unsophisticated soldier. Courtly chivalry helped to educate and humanize the knight, certainly it taught him some gentler emotions and increased perception, but it did not criticize his trade. Born in a home fortified for war, the knight advanced through life as if to martial music.

The castle, in the early days, was nothing more than a crude wooden tower. Before the clearing of the European forests, wood was universally available, and always some among the knight's tenants were able to work it; whereas the stonemason was a craftsman, expensive and rare. In the tower, a dark cavernous place set aside for stores was surmounted by a large single room in which the owner (says an eleventh-century account) 'together with his household, lived, conversed, ate, and slept'. Raised on a mound with a ditch at the foot, the tower peered over a stockaded enclosure into which flocks and tenants might escape in times of trouble. A watchman on the roof night and day lived in perpetual expectation of that trouble, and each band of strangers riding out of the silent countryside was greeted by the anxious blast of the watchman's horn.

For the castle of the knight was nearly always deep in the countryside. He lived off the manorial lands, relying on the labour of his tenants, and by instinct and conscious choice shunned the towns. In the country he felt unconstrained and independent, out of reach of his feudal overlords, the great nobles, bishops and kings, whose palaces were in the towns, and away from urban life which, in his simplicity, he despised and feared. Open spaces were his delight. Even in the Mediterranean south, with its stronger tradition of civilized behaviour and its glimmerings of knightly culture, the castle was still a rural place, dominating a long-established village, but still far from the town. The annals of a German monk relate the sad story of a lad, the son of a count, sent by his family to join a monastery.

Watchmen on the battlement walls: this crude representation gives an idea of the small size and simple plan of the early castle.

The walled life of the community soon oppressed his free spirit, and he would climb to the roof 'at least to cheer his vagrant soul with the sight of hills and fields where he might no longer roam'.

Though he craved for the freedom of the country, the knight resided in his castle among a permanent huddle of bodies. Privacy was almost unknown, and perhaps unwanted. Robert Grosseteste, the famous Bishop of Lincoln, gave it as his opinion that it was unseemly for a lord to eat alone. Friends, family, dependants, sons of nobles put into his care surrounded a lord at all times; men-at-arms, retainers and menials watched over him, even when he lay down with his wife at night; beggars, penitents, wanderers of all kinds crept under the stairs and remained there unmolested to chew on bones like mice in the wainscot.

The press of people within the castle and the freedom of the land outside both helped in the chivalric education of the knight. The arrival of the traveller, the democracy of the hall, and the easy access to the lord's ear made it a simple matter for the new ideals of the south to spread very quickly. The spring song of the troubadours, floating from the corner where the jongleur sat, struck home to the heart of the knight whose greatest joy was in country pastimes. And his joy in his land was all the keener because he himself did not have to work it. A steward had the management of the estate and a poor knight reduced to setting his hand to the plough was humiliated indeed. The recognition of the enchantment of nature by those who were constitutionally used to an outdoor life was the beginning of chivalric refinement. The chivalrous knight (as the poet of *Méon* conceived

The look-out in the castle tower, from the *Roman de Lancelot*.

Spanish *juglar* and *juglaresca*—itinerant musicians—playing a large wind instrument of the shawm family accompanied by a drum. From the *Cantigas de Sta Maria*.

The development of the medieval castle: two early stone fortresses. (*Right*) The ruins of the Château de Villandraut show the form of the battlements; (*overleaf*) the ruined donjon of the Château de Bonaguil shows the arrangement of the lord's great hall, with the large fireplace occupying one end of the apartment.

him in the true spirit of romance) rose in the summer dawn, stepped into misty fields to welcome the dew on the grass and the roses opening to the light.

A new taste, and some more wealth, brought changes in architecture. In the twelfth century spacious buildings in stone began to displace the wooden forts, even for barons of quite modest rank. Bertran de Born spoke of those rich lords who built in stone 'gateways and turrets, vaults and spiral staircases'. The romance *Gaufrey* added a poetic account of castle construction. Ten stone-cutters, twenty-five masons and over a hundred labourers worked for three and a half years. In amazement, a daily audience gathered to watch the clearing of the forest, the digging of the foundations, the erection of the scaffolding and, at last, the slow ascent of the great, grey blocks of stone. In time the massive donjon was revealed, standing on its high rock with the chapel sheltering by its side. Water sparkled in the moats, fruit ripened in the orchard, the meadows were grown, and the park stocked.

Moat and barbican, portcullis and drawbridge, crenellations and arrow-slits, the great keep with its inevitable prison-hole where many, like Ogier the Dane, were thrown with rodents and reptiles— the stone castle was obviously designed for greater strength and better defence, a baleful emblem of bad intentions. But the permanence of stone, the solidity of many vaulted chambers, and the graces

of the mason's art encouraged the more expansive life of courtly chivalry. The noisome camaraderie of the smoke-filled wooden hall was alleviated by the provision of more space and more apartments. The great hall was still the centre of castle life, but there were now one or two bedrooms also, some with adjoining ante-chambers, stores and work-rooms beneath the hall, and a spartan bathroom in the vaults for the baron's cold tub; the medieval knight, unlike a later aristocracy, was a great man for bathing. The quarters for servants and animals were now separate from the chief apartments.

And construction in stone allowed far more comfort and elegance in the appointments of the castle. Great chimneys carried the smoke away; stone flags or tessellated bricks were often preferred to bare boards; glass appeared in the windows; benches and couches were provided, skins scattered profusely, and rooms hung with curtains and tapestry. The rule for any lord of distinction was to have the interior of his castle painted. Arches, doorways, pillars and beams were picked out with contrasting bands of colour, black and red ochre and sombre yellow; the chambers themselves were boldly decorated with a multitude of birds, beasts and flowers; a room in the poem *Elie de Saint-Gilles* seemed a veritable Noah's Ark, and *Gaufrey* spoke of a palace entirely painted with flowers. Flowers, too, were haphazardly sprinkled in the baron's pleasure-grounds, planted beyond the fortifications, a shaggy enclosure of fruit trees, shrubs, roses, not neatly kept but softening the austere granite of the walls. Here, broken by the trials of war, or in the restless evenings of a long peace, the lord would come to ease a fretful mind.

Peace—the most hateful time for the knight. And the enforced peace of winter, grey days contending with grey walls, the rooms infinitely gloomy, the damp cold striking to the bone anywhere beyond the limited reach of the log fires, was the most oppressive time of all. The artifices of chivalry helped him to endure the interminable lame passage of the day. Shut off for long periods from the beloved activity of the open air, and shut off also from learned pleasures by a natural disinclination (and perhaps by illiteracy), he needed

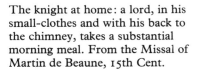
The knight at home: a lord, in his small-clothes and with his back to the chimney, takes a substantial morning meal. From the Missal of Martin de Beaune, 15th Cent.

ceremony, movement, physical occupations to beguile his boredom. Feudal rank imposed certain duties on him, but the government of tenants and the handling of the estate were usually left to bailiffs and stewards. Occasionally he sat as judge among his vassals or his peers, and in certain places, in particular England and Germany, he had a duty to defend public order beyond the borders of his own manors. And he ruled his household with a peremptory, not to say tyrannical hand.

But the duties were soon done and the day waited to be filled. Courtly chivalry attempted to transmute this dull chaos of time into a stately progression. Rising at dawn to get the benefit of all the hours of light, the knight began his day with his devotions. The strong Christian foundation of chivalry gave even the boldest predator a proper reverence at least for the forms of religion, and the early fashion of knighthood was to pray full length on the ground, with the arms spread in imitation of Christ on the cross, and the head pointing to the east. And after this prostration the knight went into Mass, very often a sung Mass. That done, he came with cheerful anticipation to the hall, for the proverb had it that 'to eat well in the morning brought good health'.

The morning passed with business, if any, or else with impatience. The curious late medieval document on the 'fifteen joys' of a knight mentioned him, crouched like a scullion, warming himself in winter 'in the chimney corner of the great fireplace'. The approach of dinner cheered him; as is usual among country-folk with little to do, food was never far from his mind. Chief among those 'fifteen joys' were 'eating heartily and making short work of the store of wine'. Meals were the pleasant oases of the day. The early knight, the unreformed warrior, had been a notorious hog, tearing haunches of meat and slobbering gallons of wine. The chivalric knight, while still a trencher-man of startling capacity, had learnt to order his meal into something more like a feast and less like a debauch. Noon was the usual hour for dining. And the meal was often stretched to great lengths: the poet of *Perceval* speaks of eight hours. Certainly on a great occasion a meal of up to ten courses was not unusual. The poets consider five pâtés and five capons (with wine to match) an adequate repast for a hero such as Renoart; and Guy de Bourgogne, in another poem,

The knight at home: preparation and service of the meal. From the Luttrell Psalter, *c.* 1340.

'A man who eats well will never be a coward.'

greatly impresses the Saracens with an appetite sufficient for four ordinary men: 'A man who eats well will never be a coward.' So the courses of fish and game and meat succeeded each other on to the table, the solid sustenance of boar and peacock and swan to be followed by the lighter fare of capon, small fowl and fish which in turn gave way to the frivolity of pastries, fruits and cheeses. The whole was washed down by wine, sometimes by cider or beer, often with spiced, aromatic meads and metheglins, known in France as *clare* and *bougleraste*.

While the knights argued (wrote the poet) 'of arms, and love, and dogs, and hawks, and tournaments and fighting', a strain of music pierced the babble, sounds of a young girl playing 'notes and lays most pleasantly'. Tunes were taken up: a drinking-song roared across the boards; the sweeter music of a love-song; or the mournful complaint of the Crusader—'Leaving the land where my dear one lives has filled me with great sadness.' The day has declined into the long winter evening. Servants stirred the fire into a great blaze. Chess or dice were sometimes produced. But the greatest happiness was to have a minstrel in the midst ready to sing the Provençal lyrics of the south, or to recite the narrative epics and romances of the north. The knight, said the 'fifteen joys', gladly kept open house 'to any wandering minstrels, heard all their songs and made music with them'.

First, an invocation to God and to his Blessed Mother, and then the jongleur began. 'Barons,' he typically demanded in the preamble to *Renaud de Montauban*: 'Barons, pray listen to me and leave your discourse. I begin, my lords, a song of knighthood, of great chivalry, and marvellous courage.' And here began the demonstrations of chivalry. Bound by music and poetry, the knight learnt of Christian virtue, of true loyalty among vassals, of strength and courage in battle, of resignation in adversity, of charity to the poor, of courtesy to strangers, of amity among companions, and of love to women. The force of these lessons depended on the extraordinary force of the minstrel's art. Did not the Conqueror give his minstrel Berdic three estates in the county of Gloucester? Did not the son of the Conqueror, that wise politician Henry I, threaten to blind the captured minstrel Luc de la Barre for composing satires against the throne? Henry II employed the poet Wace to celebrate English history, and William Longchamp hired minstrels to sing the praises of Richard Lionheart in the King's absence. The hold of the minstrel cannot be imagined in this age of books and easy reading. The great and stern fighting baron William Marshall, who on his death bed in 1219 admitted to capturing five hundred knights in his lifetime, longed but did not dare to sing in his final illness; yet he would not die until his daughters had been called and made to sing the lyrics of the troubadours, which they did somewhat nervously so that the old warrior stopped his youngest and taught her how the *retruenge* should go. By the strength of such devotion to words and music the lessons of chivalry descended from the great nobles of the south, where courtesy began, to the rude knights of Europe, a race not naturally disposed to tenderness or delicacy.

But no entertainment could quite make up for the enforced idleness of the winter. Warmer days were welcomed with relief and the impatient thoughts of a warlike aristocracy turned to hunting and tourneys, those peaceful substitutes for war. At first, hunting was as much a necessity as a pleasure for all classes of society, for food and to keep down wild beasts. But gradually the landowners excluded other hunters from their land, and the greater the landowner the greater the preserve, or 'forest', set aside solely for his own recreation. Hunting became largely a noble prerogative. This happened particularly in England where the Conqueror set the example, to the great disgust of his Anglo-Saxon subjects. 'He made large forests for deer,' said the *Anglo-Saxon Chronicle*, 'and enacted laws therewith, so that whoever killed a hart or a hind should be blinded. As he forbade killing the deer, so also the boars. And he loved the tall stags as if he were their father.' Hunting-forests were often created at the expense of arable land. But the loss to peasant farmers was of no account. So much did the nobility come to glory in hunting, they did not scruple to use all their despotic power to burden a weary tenantry with obligations to look after animals, to kennel and feed the lord's hounds, to beat up his game, and to bear home the kill.

Hawks, greyhounds, boarhounds, staghounds were all equally loved, and extraordinary pains were taken for their training and welfare. A count of Guines was said to set 'greater store by a goshawk beating the air with its wings than by a priestly sermon'. A fourteenth-century French treatise recommended, for the training of a hawk, that 'you must keep him on your fist more than ever before, taking him to law-courts and among folk assembled in church or elsewhere, and into the streets'. Churchmen and nuns of noble birth still clung to their hunting-animals. A fourteenth-century bishop's visitation to three genteel nunneries in the south of England found 'hunting-dogs and other hounds abiding within your monastic precinct' consuming the alms that should have gone to the poor. The household book of Westminster Abbey recorded, in 1368, 3d. spent on a collar for Sturdy, the Lord Abbot's greyhound. The pandering to animals, the bringing of yapping dogs and hooded hawks to church (complained a later German cleric) was very blameworthy in all men, 'but most blameworthy in the clergy, though some would fain excuse themselves on the plea of noble birth'.

If the Church disliked hunting, it abominated tourneys, those dangerous imitations of war. Nothing demonstrates the uneasy Christianity of chivalry so well as the implacable opposition between Church and knight on the question of tournaments. To the Church, they were merely a continuation of those deadly 'pagan games' which early chronicles spoke of, wild outbursts of barbaric energy that saw the death of many young men. Church authority always considered the tourney 'an execrable and accursed game'; Pope Innocent II, at the Council of Clermont in 1130, forbade them 'because they often cost a man his life', and the Council denied a church burial to those killed in the lists. St Bernard, the great advocate of crusading warfare, fulminated against the sinful waste of tourneys and advised Abbot Suger to 'take up the sword of the spirit, that is to say, the

The knight at home: the death-bed scene. From the *Book of Hours* of Catherine de Cleves (Flemish, c. 1435).

Hunting with falcons. The lord returns from the hunt and carefully hands his birds to his servants. The popularity of falconry, chiefly for entertainment but also to supply food, made the birds highly prized. From a *Treatise of Falconry* by the sophisticated and pleasure-loving Emperor Frederick II.

Word of God, against these inventions of the devil which take new root among men'. Jacques de Vitry, always the enemy of pride and the friend of the poor, spoke of the vicious blows of the combat, the shame and the wounds of the vanquished, the coarse triumph of the victor; he spoke of harvests ruined by rampaging knights, of tenants crushed by the intolerable taxes needed to support the great expense of a tournament, and, at last, of the debauched feasting after a tourney which led many times to further blows and sometimes to homicide. The ingenuous monastic writer Robert Manning, in his late thirteenth-century poem *Handlyng Synne*, found 'seven points of deadly sin' in tournaments: pride in one's strength, envy of others, wrath in the combat, sloth in placing pleasure before devotion, covetousness of the opponent's horse and equipment, finally gluttony at the feast and lechery afterwards.

To the knight, early tournaments, the bloody affrays that went under the name of 'pagan games', were simply a necessary part of training in the art of war; and the tourney always retained something of this function. 'For the use of young knights, as it were to make them all to fight in battle,' wrote the chronicler Ralph Higden under the year 1195, 'that time tournaments, that were left of long time, were made and used again, not withstanding the pope's forbidding.' But one of the effects of chivalry was the transformation of feudal necessity into courtly pleasure, and it is no surprise that later ages dated (quite wrongly) the invention of the tournament roughly from the beginning of chivalry, in the mid-eleventh century, and credited the invention (perhaps rightly) to France: to Matthew Paris, writing his English chronicle in St Albans, the tourney was a 'French conflict'.

Chivalry changed the brutal mêlée of an earlier age into a kind of superior entertainment, a sporting contest blending trials of strength and skill with pageantry and festivity; it became the favourite amusement of the warlike nobility. The transformation was gradual. An early distinction was made between the 'tournament' and the 'joust', the former resembling a miniature war between bands, and the latter being single combat between champions. In both types of competition the fighting was still severe. William Marshall, an indefatigable enthusiast who fought twice a month in his youth, being declared the victor on one occasion, was discovered in the blacksmith's shop having the battered helmet prised from his head; and as late as 1240, between sixty and eighty combatants were killed at a certain tourney. Some hundred years later Froissart still spoke of *joustes mortelles.*

The evolution of tourneys made them formal and gallant exercises rather than preparation for war. Because of very great expense only kings and the richest nobles could afford to hold them; a tournament became an extravagant adjunct to great court occasions. Young knights wandered the land in search of these occasions, grouped into 'companies' (or teams) according to nationality, the high-born youth seeking fame and the poor knight hoping for the spoils of victory: it was a rule of the contest that the vanquished

Harold and Duke William ride together. William carries his falcon, a hunting-bird to which the medieval lord was so greatly attached. A scene from the Bayeux Tapestry.

forfeited horse and equipment, even the person of the loser was sometimes held to ransom. The practice of jousting could be a lucrative profession, and greed was a dangerous spur to men who were normally only too ready to quarrel. Pretensions of gallantry, the ladies in the stands, champions in gorgeous armour, emblems and pennants flying, music and dancing and feasting, all contrasted starkly with the grim intention of the combatants, dealing cruel and serious blows, gladly stripping the armour from the fallen warrior whose life-blood had drained away into the sands of the lists. Wise monarchs condemned tourneys as heartily as the Church had done. Henry II forbade them in England; in France, Philip Augustus bound his sons by oath never to take part, and St Louis damned them as dangerous frivolities.

79

Courtly chivalry put the gloss of sophistication on the feudal life, substituting for some of the epic hardness the romantic expectation of delight. The nature of the knight was not changed, but his responsibilities were diminished. The old knight was active in a desperate cause, to protect the very existence of his society, and dangers left him no time to be anything other than the brutal warrior that he was. The success of these first feudal knights left a most doubtful inheritance to their chivalrous descendants. John of Salisbury, clearest and soundest of medieval critics, noted this. Castigating the courtiers of Henry II in his *Policraticus*, he wrote: 'Success, implacable foe of virtue, applauds its devotees only to harm them, and with its ill-starred prosperity escorts them on their joyous way to bring about their ultimate fall by first pledging them in cups of sweet wine and, when they are intoxicated thereby, mixing in the draught deadly poison or something conceivably worse. The more brilliant the success the denser the clouds that gather around their dazzled eyes. As the darkness thickens truth vanishes, virtue withers with severed roots, and a crop of vices sprouts.'

Was not this the case of the chivalrous knight? Full of restlessness, of boundless energy and demanding physical activity, but no longer fully occupied by war, he had no function but to amuse himself and so dashed into the distractions that courtly chivalry offered. One of the romances anatomized the life of the knight as 'dice and other games, and jousting and dancing and carolling all the year round, and greeting fools and jesters and minstrels and jongleurs'. The pursuit of pleasure, John of Salisbury warned, was no way to reach virtue. 'I am not speaking', he continued, eyeing the brawny young loiterers of chivalry, 'of the pleasure which is the fruit of peace, patience, kindness, forbearance, and delight in the spirit of holiness. I refer to pleasure which, devoted to feasting, drinking, banquets, songs and dances, sport, over-refinements of luxury, debauchery, and varied types of defilement, weakens even robust souls.' The knightly search for entertainment was uncritical and tempestuous, delighting the body more than the mind, and indulged by men of strong appetites naturally led to excess. Prodigal irrationality marked too many chivalrous occasions, such as the one at Beaucaire in 1177, recorded by the chronicler Geoffroi de Vigeois. Here, one knight ploughed the lanes of the castle with a yoke of oxen and sowed the furrows with pieces of silver; another cooked for his retinue of three hundred on wax candles; and another had thirty horses burnt alive for a boast. In the formation of chivalry, pagan indulgence vied dangerously with Christian idealism.

*Opposite, top.* The encampment of Guidoriccio da Fogliano, by Simone Martini (1284–1344).

*Opposite, bottom.* The knight at home: courtly scene in an Italian bed-chamber, with games of skill and love.

# chapter four

Men do not live without women, though some ages pretend they could do so. Early laws in the west gave woman scant acknowledgement: early society, at least in its official voice, gave her little respect. A parcel of ecclesiastical misogynists, repeating with indecent enthusiasm the criticisms of St Jerome, had written her down. She was Eve, *ianua diaboli*, the devil's instrument. Cardinal Jacques de Vitry, a man in all other respects kindly and enlightened, wrote even at the height of chivalry: 'Between Adam and God in Paradise there was but one woman; yet she had no rest until she had succeeded in banishing her husband from the garden of delights and in condemning Christ to the torments of the cross.' That was insult in the grand clerical tradition, part of the tedious chronicle of self-righteous male prejudice which women bore, the sort of thing that Chaucer's Wife of Bath heard with mighty indignation from her fifth husband day after day as he droned on with his readings from his book of 'wikked wyves': sour tales from old Tertullian and Jerome, groans from the Bible against women, stories of men undone, of Samson, Hercules, Agamemnon, of the bestial lust of Pasiphae who coupled with a white bull, or of the nagging of Xantippe who emptied the piss-pot on the philosophic head of her husband Socrates. 'For trusteth well,' cried the exasperated feminist of Bath, 'it is an impossible that any clerk will speak good of wives.'

Nor did the institutions of feudalism have much care for women.

*Above*. Exchange of rings between a lady and her lover, in the presence of a chaperone. From the *Oeuvres* of Guillaume de Machaut.

*Right*. The celebration of marriage, from a 14th Cent devotional treatise.

Feudalism was a military discipline, designed for protection, and as women did not fight they had a low place in the arrangement—bearers of children (preferably male), keepers of the hearth perhaps, but disposable according to the social and warlike needs of the knight. A lovely girl was a fine thing no doubt, but many put a greater value on a helm, a horse, a good sword. 'Look Girbers,' says a character in *Girbers de Metz*, 'look at that beauty.' 'You would do better', replies the hero, 'to look at the beautiful beast of a horse I have here.'

Feudal marriage was based on convenience, and the rights of family very often took second place to the duties of a vassal. A daughter, being useless for war, was important only as a means to placate an enemy, reward a friend, or bind an alliance; and consequently a girl was hurried away at the earliest possible moment to the man chosen for her. 'Once', the author of *Aiol* lamented, 'men married only at thirty or later, and the bride would be of age. Now they arrange marriages between children of twelve.' And these crude expressions of self-interest were not absolutely repugnant to the women themselves, for no woman could afford to be unprotected amid feudal discord. In the famous poem of *El Cid*, the daughters of the hero thank their father for choosing their husbands, though they have never seen the men: 'When you have married us,' they say, 'we shall be great ladies.' The literature is full of women, single or widowed, anxious for the protection of a strong husband. 'My father died two months ago,' a young girl petitions Charlemagne in one poem. 'I request you to find me a husband.' 'My husband is dead,' says the Duchess of Burgundy in another. 'Find me a new powerful husband, for I need one to protect my lands.'

A great lord was only too eager to help the widows of his vassals to a useful remarriage, though the Church discouraged second and third unions. A fief without a knight, with only a widow to control it, was unlikely to perform the military duties owed to the suzerain. Church disapproval counted for little among the nobility; feudal practicality demanded that a well-born woman should never be without a husband. 'Be quiet,' says Garin li Loherains to his sister-in-law, weeping over her murdered husband, 'some knight will marry you, while I must continue to mourn this death.' The first reflection of Joinville, commenting on the death of six knights at Mansura in Egypt, is that six wives will need new husbands. Noble indifference to Church opinion and to a woman's heart went further. Marriage was a sacrament that could not be dissolved, yet repudiations and divorces, for reasons of policy, were common enough in great families. John, Marshal of England, married a lass of singular beauty and dignity and charm, and had 'great joy' with her. He then discovered a need to placate a powerful and dangerous neighbour, so putting aside his first lovely wife he married the sister of the neighbour.

What right (the male world implied) did a woman have to moan? If she had rank and property some knight would always take her up. Let her remain in the quietness of the home where her honour and reputation were easily preserved. A knight, Philippe de Novaire explained to the women of the thirteenth century, needed many

Wife-beating by a jealous husband; the kind of violence that women might expect in the Middle Ages. From a 14th Cent manuscript of the *Roman de la Rose*.

*Overleaf, top.* Medieval minstrels—jongleurs—and their instruments: (*a*) two vielles; (*b*) pipes and drums; (*c*) a Moor and a Christian both playing lutes; (*d*) pastoral double flute; (*e*) two shawms; (*f*) two bagpipes; (*g*) psaltery; (*h*) rebec and lute; (*i*) two transverse flutes; (*j*) carillon. From the *Cantigas Sta Maria*. (*k*). Meister Heinrich Frauenlob as king of the minstrels: the instruments played by the band are drum, flute, shawm, fiddle, psaltery and bagpipes. From the Manesse Codex, early 14th Cent. (*l*). Musicians and dancers perform before the king, in honour of the Virgin. From the *Cantigas de Alfonso el Sabio.*

a

b

c

d

e

f

g

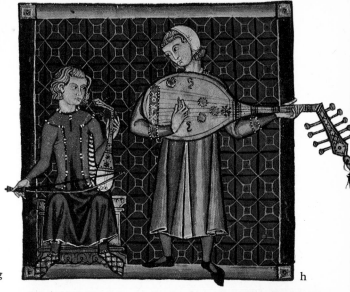

h

i

j

k

l

85

The 14th Cent feminist and author Christine de Pisan, in a group with noblemen. From a 15th Cent manuscript.

qualities to be virtuous, 'for it behoves him to be courteous and generous, brave and wise'; but a woman, 'if she be a worthy woman of her body, all her other faults are covered and she can go where she pleases with a high head'. Let her, therefore, look to her body and not meddle elsewhere. No proper man needed her opinion. 'Unhappy the noble', says the poem *Renaud de Montauban*, 'who goes to the lady's chamber for advice.' Consequently there was no need for a girl to be taught much, and any sign of female forwardness required sharp discipline. A reasonable beating was generally allowed; as late as the fourteenth century, the knight La Tour Landry advised his daughters that wives of gentlemen might expect to be knocked to the ground by their husbands.

'Who painted the lion?' the Wife of Bath demanded: who was responsible for the black portrait of women? Men made the laws, framed the feudal customs, and wrote the books. A wise person would be mad, said Chaucer's indomitable housewife, to take men's words, specially those of celibate churchmen, for the true world of women. 'By God, if women had written stories,' she justly cried, 'they would

unlikely tale, said the bewildered Usama, was 'I swear if you do it again I shall take you to court!' Another Frank, a knight, was so thunderstruck by the eastern custom of shaving pubic hair that first he had his own vigorous thatch cut off and then brought his wife to the bath-house and had her shaved before the male company, to the great shame of the Moslem bath-attendant. Usama regarded the first crusaders with the wonder of a gentleman surprised by barbarians; he saw them without jealousy or honour, 'yet at the same time they have the courage that as a rule springs only from the sense of honour and a readiness to take offence'.

The Arabs, however, recognized only too well the stout sexual appetite of the crusaders, and the elegant rhetorician Imad ad-Din devoted several fanciful pages to elucidate the mysteries of the Christian camp-followers who accompanied the Third Crusade. Three hundred lovely girls, he wrote, came from beyond the sea and offered themselves for sin; and they glowed with ardour for carnal intercourse: 'They were all licentious harlots, proud and scornful, who took and gave, foul-fleshed and sinful, singers and coquettes, appearing proudly in public, tinted and painted, who ripped open and patched up, lacerated and mended, urged and seduced, like tipsy adolescents, making love and selling themselves for gold, pink-faced and unblushing, with nasal voices and fleshy thighs, blue-eyed and grey-eyed, broken down little fools. Each one trailed the train of her robe behind her and bewitched the beholder with her effulgence. She swayed like a sapling, revealed herself like a strong castle, quivering like a small branch, walked proudly with a cross on her breast, sold her graces for gratitude, and longed to lose her robe and her honour.' Trade was brisk as 'they took the parched man's sinews to the well, and welcomed birds into the nest of their thighs'.

It was appropriate that the mild pornography of Ovid should be the favourite reading of a ruttish age, and appropriate also that men of simple lust should accept quite candidly the elegant fooling of the Roman sophisticate. The *Art of Love* was the foremost handbook on seduction, a subject that knights were keen to study. And no one was more anxious to learn the subtle arts of persuading a woman to bed than the troubadour of the Languedoc. The men of the south, it seems, out-ran their northern fellows in desire, as they did in so much else.

Beyond the mysteries of human behaviour, some reasons may be advanced for this state of affairs. The Church was relatively weak in the south, and her servants too often no advertisement for holiness. 'Vultures and kites', wrote the troubadour Peire Cardinal, 'scent not rotting flesh so well as priests and friars sniff the houses of the rich.' The whole organization of the Church brought from Cardinal a magnificent and typical southern scorn: 'The priests call themselves shepherds, but in truth they are murderers; they have the look of holiness in their clothing, but they remind me of Sir Wolf who, for fear of the dogs, entered the fold in sheep's clothing, beguiled the silly sheep and ate them all up.' Where the clergy were not respected, the ideals of the Church were ignored. The Church taught an ascetic ideal, but the clergy were seen to couple and marry and keep concu-

The rule of love: Tristram, Lancelot and other devotees pay homage to Venus. Italian tray, *c.* 1400.

The lover and his lady, from the
*Roman de la Rose*, 14th Cent.

bines. Why should not the laity also break the hard rules that circum-
scribed Christian relations, rules that absolutely forbade any sexual
act outside marriage and declared any desire beyond the needs of
procreation guilty even in marriage? In the fragmented petty fiefdoms of the south there were many unattached knights with no
property or rank to attract a lady, and many unattached ladies without hope of finding a lord sufficiently worthy to please their fathers.
The advice of the libertine Ovid, who made no distinction between
married and unmarried, was distinctly needed and fully appreciated.
The south was notoriously pleasure-seeking. The northern crusaders, stern practitioners of military chivalry, considered the
southern knights rather unmanly—'French to the wars, Provençals
to the feast', as an old proverb had it. A land that had, in the words of
the troubadours, greeted so ardently the advent of spring and the
beauties of nature was open to the darts of desire.

No one could mistake the intention of the early troubadours. 'May
God grant', implored William of Poitiers in one of his love poems,
'that I live long enough to have my hands beneath her cloak.' The
swift current of lust, the powerful undertow of primitive sexuality,
stated so plainly by William of Poitiers, first of the troubadours,
surged beneath all troubadour protestations on love. 'How many
times did I tumble them?' William joyfully boasted in another ribald
poem. 'A hundred and eighty-eight to be precise, so that I almost
broke my girth and harness.' The earthy vigour was taken up by
William's immediate successors. 'I cannot stay or live', wrote
Cercamon, reckoned the second troubadour, 'unless she is naked by
my side, to kiss and clasp in a hidden room.' The misanthropic
Marcabrun, the third of the Provençal poets, accepted that this

business between men and women was little more than a goatish mounting brought on by an incurable itch. 'You goat-like husbands have invaded the bed and made the cunt a thief,' was his bitter comment. 'And since I, Marcabrun, see you like it that way, I'll merely say that in this skin game husbands get fleeced instead of shaven.' And he considered this depravity a particular mark of his own times: 'Perhaps love was once dear, but now it has turned vile, and virginity is a thing past.'

After the early crudities, when troubadours began to dress desire more elegantly, the courtly poets were still not embarrassed to admit that a lusting body enclosed the most swooning heart. Bernart de Ventadorn, whose delicate art is a far cry from the coarse ranting of the first troubadour, wrote: 'May she have the courage to welcome me one night in her privy room, and make me a necklace of her arms.' Bernart moulded the rustic humpings of William of Poitiers into a more lascivious sensuality which was to become one characteristic of troubadour style. 'I'll surely die of longing and desire', Bernart sighed, 'if that beauty does not call me to her bed, to let me caress and kiss her, and press against me her white, smooth, soft body.' And women, on the evidence of Provençal poems, also accepted the satisfaction of the body as the chief end of knightly love. 'No one can ever know', said a lady, reflecting tenderly on her distant lover, 'my secret solace, imagining him lying in my arms until his image vanishes.' That was a poetic fiction of Peire d'Auvergne, but his words were echoed almost exactly by the noble poetess, the Countess of Die: 'How I wish to hold him one night in my naked arms and see him joyfully use my body as a pillow.' 'Oh, that I might lie with you one night', she addressed her lover with passionate directness, 'and caress you lovingly.'

Lover's lust was better than warrior's neglect. A mutual joy in the flesh was a recognition of women, for there was an equality between the sexes in the giving and taking of pleasure. But the influence of the troubadours was always to civilize the gross emotions, and by slow steps, in the course of the twelfth century, they transmuted lust into romance. In their poetry they devised a strange declension of love bound by rules and expectations that were entirely new to the west. The first impulse, so many think, came from the Arab kingdoms of the Spanish peninsula. In the century preceding the First Crusade, the small Moslem courts of Spain were politically divided, but each with a flourishing culture. The support of poetry was the duty of the Arab prince and each court, sometimes each village, had its appointed poet whose position was of such dignity that the poet was often sent to Arabia to learn the authentic classical tradition. On his return, the poet celebrated, not the dryness of the Arabian Desert, but the sweetness of Andalusian gardens, sun and shade, running water and fruits, and all manner of attendant delights.

The Moslem principalities were havens of learning, culture and ease to which Christian Europe could offer nothing in comparison. Around 1050 the petty Moorish court of Almeria could boast a library of some four hundred thousand manuscripts; the largest library in the Christian north of Spain could claim no more than

The troubadour Bernart de Ventadorn. The picture makes it plain that Bernart was not only a poet, but also a musician and performer of his own lyrics.

Music and chess played by ladies of a Spanish court. The courts of northern Spain, in touch with the Moorish kingdoms, were one of the chief means for transmitting Arab culture to Europe: both the lute and the game of chess originated in the East. From a *Treatise on Chess* by Alfonso the Wise, *c.* 1283.

two hundred volumes. Communication between Moor and Christian was easy and familiar, for until the arrival of the Almoravid dynasty from North Africa in 1086 there was no fanaticism among the Moslems. The Arab poets were also court functionaries and they wandered freely about the Christian states around the Pyrenees on embassies and diplomatic missions, scattering widely their poetry and ideas in a way very similar to the practice of the troubadours a century later. Nor was there a great difficulty with language, for once again the people of these early centuries showed their confidence in handling foreign tongues. We know from Usama ibn Munqidh that ignorant Frankish knights of the First Crusade quickly picked up Arabic, and it is certain that many Christians bordering on Moslem states were bilingual. King Pedro of Aragon, stepson of William of Poitiers, would sign Latin documents in Arabic, 'Pedro ibn Sancho'. The forms of Arabic verse have been noted in the lyric poetry of the troubadours.

With the forms came also a certain content that was new. The luxurious and refined airs of southern Spain had produced a Moorish view of women and love that was startlingly different from the hearty, friendly sexuality of the Christian nobility. The Moorish ideal, expressed in such works as *The Dove's Neck-Ring* written by Ali ibn Hazm around 1022, though recognizing the joy of the body, sought rather the union of souls. Love was not a cheerful, sweaty tussle, but an ennobling experience that made 'a mean one generous, a gloomy one happy, a coward brave, the bad-tempered gay, the ignorant clever, the slovenly smart, and the ugly handsome'. Love was jealous and possessive, abject and anxious. Whether the beloved was countess or servant-girl, the lover was as a slave before her and addressed her as *sayyidi* or *mawlaya*—'my lord' or 'my master': 'I have trodden the carpets of khalifs,' wrote ibn Hazm, 'and I never saw a timid respect which would equal that of a lover before his beloved.' The submissive lover found joy in the least kindness, and even a sort of contentment in rejection; ibn Ammar expressed this paradox when he wrote that love's delights were made of its burning torments.

How astounding all this was to feudal knights, that they should humble themselves to, or deign to be jealous of mere women! The strangeness of this doctrine caused the Moorish lore of courtesy to cross the Pyrenees haltingly and with modifications. The Moslem ideal quite definitely preferred chaste to sensual love, and stated emphatically that a lover's devotion was not to be offered to a married woman. But the hot-blooded knights were not keen on continence, and somehow, in the northern version of courtesy, the amoral and sensual rules of the old favourite Ovid were mixed with the purer devotion of the Moorish tradition. For Ovid also had advocated humility, an ironical submission to a lady's whims as a means to creep into her bed. Leave your business, said Ovid, and humbly await her, hour after hour, in the street; run errands without complaint; escort her from balls and feasts; take her, at the least com-

A lady rescued from brigands. From the *Histoire du St Graal* by Robert de Boron.

poteris si iusticie ñ trellexeris i facie 2muta fall

Dances in a garden, from the *Songs of Paris*, 14th Cent.

mand, on a country tour, though the sun burns or snow falls: 'Our general, Love, disdains a lukewarm service in his long campaigns.' Knights were set on penetrating the lady's defences, and Ovid showed a dissembling way to undermine the barriers. His ironic rules of humility and service became a serious part of courtly behaviour.

By an adroit mixture of Roman, Arab and Christian sources (and no doubt by some misunderstanding of each), the troubadours arrived at their own version of proper conduct in love. The elements of the new doctrine were courtesy, humility, adultery, and a religious devotion to the beloved.

These elements, from diverse sources and in strange conjunction, were all a reflection or expression of the feudal life of the knight. Courtly love, though quite unlike anything that had been seen before in a Christian country, was still love in a feudal aspect. Courtesy expressed the civilized manner and conduct of courtiers who benefited from the learning and refinement that grew up round the person of the king or the great feudal noble. The humility of the lover was an

The ladies of the Court of Idleness. From a 14th Cent Italian Treatise on the Vices.

easy displacement of the feudal reverence and loyalty that the vassal gave to his lord; to look on the lady as a feudal superior was to obey her, and in many cases, especially when the lover was a troubadour, the beloved was indeed of higher rank than the man. The lively image of love as warfare, used by Ovid among others, was well understood by knights, who knew the trials of a campaign. The reasons for courtesy and humility were plain to see; but a more peculiar contemporary logic encouraged adultery and religious parody.

Since marriages among the knightly class were arranged according to political and family interests, with no consideration for the hearts of the betrothed, no strong emotion was likely to be aroused in marriage. With a practical determination to make the best of circumstances, the partners often achieved a kind of friendly companionship. But passion was no part of the consideration, for the parents who decided the match or for the husband and wife who submitted to it. A love that was freely given, ardent, demanding, had to be outside matrimony; passion seemed to be naturally adulterous. Moreover, the Church, though having nothing to say on romantic love (since she had never heard of it before the troubadours elaborated their doctrine in the twelfth century), took a very severe view of all sexuality. Sex was for procreation, and while not sinful in itself, it was to be used, like a too-powerful drug, with suspicion and moderation. Some theologians regretted the whole business and contended that, in a state of innocence, we would be generated 'without the incentive of the flesh'. Other theologians quoted with approval the ancient maxim that 'passionate love of one's own wife was adultery'. There was, therefore, a persuasive opinion that the kind of love advocated by the courtly poets was wicked even in marriage, and so these poets, condemned from the start, with a sort of bravado deliberately emphasized the adulterous nature of their passion.

The elevation of the beloved into a goddess, one of the most characteristic features of courtly chivalry, began perhaps with the sentimental and exaggerated awe that Arab courtesy recommended for romantic lovers. The early troubadour Jaufre Rudel spoke of the *princesse lointaine*, the far-distant lady whom the lover aspired to, but might hardly reach. Ovid, in his playful erotic art, had made Love a god. His courtly followers had soon deified the 'far-distant lady', and, with more imagination than taste, began to give her some of the veneration due to the Virgin Mary. Whether this was a real confusion of images, or a shocking parody of religion, is by no means certain. The Middle Ages were notoriously uncritical and even less able than ourselves to understand their true motives. There was the deliberate insolence of parody in such works as the twelfth-century *Council of Remiremont*, where a chapter of nuns are regulated by the Rule of Ovid, hymn the god of love, and debate, before a female cardinal, the respective sexual merits of knights or clergy, deciding in favour of the latter. And there was a brave desperation in Aucassin's cry, in the famous tale of *Aucassin and Nicolette*, that he would follow sweet ladies and goodly knights to hell rather than go to heaven without them: that was a proclamation of the rights of romantic love against the narrow sexual view of the Church. But when Bernart de Ventadorn, suavest of troubadours, in the same verse raised his hands to heaven and lowered his eyes to the girdle, was he blasphemous or innocent? 'Lady, for your love I join hands and worship you. Soft body with scented skin, what grief you bring me!' Certainly the cult of the Virgin was particularly strong, and her radiance illuminated her fellow women: 'Our blessed Lady', wrote an anonymous poet, 'beareth the name of all women wherever they go.'

The game of love required the participation of the lady; without her acceptance of the romantic lead the play could not be done. Men elaborated the chivalric code, but romance (as its advocates were the first to insist) bloomed only by the kindly light of woman's eyes. Courtly love was an unacknowledged accomplishment of women; it was perhaps their first triumph in the Christian west. At the time of the First Crusade the apprehensive churchman Guibert de Nogent saw the women at their devilish work, wantonly dressed, with immodest laughter and brazen display. Each woman, he noted, 'thinks she has plunged the depths of misery if she lack lovers, and measures her nobility and courtliness by the number of her suitors'.

In the courts of southern France the poets of the new devotion met the women worthy of their songs. Count William, troubadour and salty philanderer, wore his mistress's device on his shield, an effective demonstration of courtly regard which other southern nobles found delightfully improper. Once called to the attention, the starry points of feminine grace began to shine in the surly dark of feudalism. In courts such as that of Ebles II of Ventadorn, himself a troubadour and a friend of William of Poitiers, noblewomen began to exact the service that poets were ready to give them. Bernart, who stoked the castle ovens at Ventadorn until his poetic gifts brought him within the court, wrote of 'the school of Ebles' which celebrated the glory of women. Intoxicated with the eloquence of his own songs, the low-born Bernart (says the *Lives of the Troubadours*) gave his heart to his lord's wife, and the Viscountess returned his passion, causing her to be locked up and him to be banished; for the romantic code of adultery, so entertaining in courtly poetry, was abominable when directed to one's own wife, and the inevitable consequence of troubadour sentiment was to uncage jealousy, that old rampaging beast.

With the bravery of poetic conviction the troubadours enrolled themselves in the dangerous service of high-born ladies, and seemed deliberately to squander their love on those socially far beyond them. From the picturesque *Lives* we learn that Guiraudon the Red, poor knight of Toulouse, loved the daughter of Alfonso, his lord; that Jaufre Rudel loved the Countess of Tripoli, took the crusader's cross for her sake, sickened and died in her arms; that Guillem of Cabestaing, giving his heart to the lady of Castel-Roussillon, had that same tender organ cut out by her cruel husband, cooked and served to the lady; that Peire Rogier loved the great patroness Ermengarde of Narbonne who looked on him favourably and made

Effigy of Queen Eleanor of
Aquitaine.

him prosper; that Arnaut of Marvoil loved the Countess of Béziers,
and thus won the jealous enmity of King Alfonso. And the writers
of the *Lives* lead us interminably through the despairing passions
of many another troubadour.

The incidents of these biographies are not to be taken as historical
truths, but they all imply the great truth, which is confirmed by the
poetry, that the troubadours, whether platonically, playfully or in
earnest, put heart and inspiration under the tutelage of noblewomen.
All acts of chivalry were ultimately consummated by the lady's
approval. 'By God's bonnet,' said the Count of Soissons in high
excitement to Joinville, chopping among the Saracens at the battle of
Mansura, 'you and I shall yet talk of this day's work in ladies' chambers.' In return for his devotion, a proper courtly knight had the
sympathetic consideration of the lady, and perhaps a hint of a
promise of love fulfilled. The historical role of Ermengarde of
Narbonne, who ruled her lands from 1143 to 1192 was exactly that
assigned to her by the *Lives*: the great friend to courtly poetry and a
lady most respectfully and lovingly fêted by the troubadours. No
one knows if Bernart's love for the Viscountess of Ventadorn went as
far as the poet so achingly desired, but we do know from his poems
that she was his '*Bel Vezer*' (his 'Lovely Vision'), the inspiration
of his passionate lyrics, and that after leaving Ventadorn (whether
banished or otherwise) the poet gave his devotion to an even greater
lady, none other than Eleanor of Aquitaine, and was repaid with
kindliness.

If Ermengarde was the patroness of the south, Eleanor was the
missionary to the north, including courtly love among the mixed
baggage of conflicting ideals that she lugged about on her various

political and matrimonial forays. As the grand-daughter of William of Poitiers, as the Queen first of France and then of England (but always Duchess of Aquitaine in her own right), as the most wilful and powerful woman of her day, she was by far the fittest woman to carry the code of the troubadours into the suspicious north. France resisted at first. By 1154, having cast off Louis and been remarried to the more sprightly Henry, Eleanor found herself Queen of England, where courtly ideals were better received. France eventually gave way under the grand alliance of Eleanor and her numerous off-spring. Her English sons, Henry, Geoffrey and Richard Lionheart, filled their mother's ancestral lands round Poitiers with southern poets whose songs, investing the boundary of the French dominions, quietly filtered north. Her daughters by the French King, Marie and Alix, boldly attacked the heart of France. When Marie married Henry of Champagne and Alix married Thibaut of Blois, both in 1164, they brought their courts under the influence of the trouvère (the French follower of the Provençal troubadour), and raised courtly love to its most elegant expression, somewhat purged of the cruder aspect of southern lust.

The seeds of courtesy which Eleanor took from the lyric poetry of her native Languedoc ripened in the northern courts of her family, in Rouen, in London, in Troyes, and were harvested by the French-speaking writers of narrative romance. The true infancy of King Arthur, Lancelot, all those goodly knights and fair ladies, was spent not on some mythical coast of Britain or Wales, but in the courts of Eleanor and her children. For ensnared in politics as she was, Eleanor remembered her poets. The times went bad for Henry and her. She retreated to her own lands south of the Loire and set her sons against their father. Her family, said a chronicler, became troubled 'like that of Oedipus'. But about 1170 she went to her own city of Poitiers and in defiance, perhaps in derision, of her husband set up her own court faithful to the precepts of courtly manners.

The court that gathered round the ducal hall at Poitiers was a very southern assembly, necessitous knights, landless young squires, a clutch of demoiselles of a marriageable age but as yet unpaired, a bewildering warren of children, adventurers, brawlers, poets, singers, a sporting, litigious, amorous crew, without the sobriety or nationalism of the north, united chiefly in a typical southern search for pleasure. The rulers of this court were the matriarch Eleanor and her eldest daughter Marie of Champagne, dispatched by her French father to keep an eye on French interests and also to help Eleanor with the preparation and schooling of the many royal progeny that sheltered behind the august skirts of the great Queen. Marie, a serene woman in her late twenties, was the very best person to bring graceful order among this hectic southern rabble. She shared her mother's courtly tastes without having the Queen's turbulent ambition. And she was deeply versed in the rites of courtesy, a notable patroness in her own Champagne of all that was new and startling in poetry and manners.

The first evidence of Marie's guidance was an increase in smartness and luxury which the chronicler noted and disapproved. 'Time was',

*Above.* A train of royal ladies. From the Luttrell Psalter, *c.* 1340.

*Opposite.* Cupid at work amid the lovers in the garden. From a 14th Cent ivory mirror-case.

wrote Geoffroi de Vigeois, 'when great men were content to go in sheep and fox skins. Now the humblest would blush to be seen in these poor things. Now they have clothes of rich and precious stuff, coloured to suit their humours. Garments are slashed and snipped to display the linings, so that the wearers look like the devils we see in paintings.' Insolent youths (the critic continued) 'affect long hair and shoes with pointed toes', while damnable women looked like vipers 'judging by the tails they drag after them'. The little wicked luxuries, gold wreaths, brooches, rings, mirrors, comfort-boxes, girdles, gloves, tassels, were the small change of lovers.

For Marie of Champagne made love the binding of the court. The words of the old rogue Ovid were about once more, whispering indelicacies into impressionable ears. To entertain fractious courtiers and to instruct them in courtesy, Marie imitated an older practice of the Languedoc and instituted 'courts of love', which parodied the familiar feudal assemblies of liege-lord and vassals, disputed the rights of love rather than the rights of feudal service, and were governed by a great lady rather than a great lord. And the laws administered by these courts of love were drawn up and exemplified in the works of the poets, writing under the express orders of Countess Marie herself, as her poet Chrétien admitted.

The sophistication of the code of courtly love in the court of Poitiers, during the three or four years it lasted, may be studied in the works of Chrétien de Troyes. *Erec*, written before Marie arrived at her husband's town of Troyes, was remarkable only as a tale of love, a topic that would not have occurred to the earlier writers of the *chansons de geste*. But *Erec* was emphatically not about courtly love. The lovers of *Erec* are married, and wedded moreover according to a sound feudal arrangement between groom and bride's father. The lady is properly silent. And the tale continues with the casual brutality and jaunty male arrogance of the old heroic tradition. The hero Erec is so far from courtesy that he willingly lets his wife watch and hold the horse all night while he lies at ease beneath the cloak taken from her back. With the coming of Marie, the poet advanced in courtesy. He studied Ovid, translated the *Art of Love*, and incorporated some of the Roman sensuality in the romance of *Cligès*. The removal of the court to Poitiers marked a great change, for here Chrétien's *Lancelot* was written, as the poet tells us plainly, with subject-matter and manner of treatment dictated by Countess Marie.

The smooth verse of *Lancelot* is the celebration of the illicit love between the hero and Queen Guinevere, conducted according to the strictest rules of courtly devotion, with humility, courtesy, adultery and the religion of love well to the fore. One moment of hesitation in the service of his beloved costs Lancelot dearly. His life is made a misery of expiatory trials and humiliations. He is commanded to sham cowardice at a tourney and does so humbly, to the jeers of the onlookers: 'My thanks to her,' is his gallant reply, 'if she wills it so.' His love, which in fact ends with the carnal satisfactions of adultery, he still regards with religious awe. Lancelot, the courteous knight who never passes a church without dismounting and uttering a prayer, also kneels in adoration before the bed of his beloved and genuflects as he leaves her chamber. The haughty doxy who grants his most intimate desires receives the devotion properly given to the Virigin Mary.

Chrétien found some parts of Marie's code distasteful. He left *Lancelot* unfinished, and in later romances modified or neglected certain points of courtly devotion. But his work was boldly done and the romantic image of King Arthur's court stamped for all time, the court of secret love and abject service, the court of chivalry *par excellence.*

The evidence of *Lancelot* is clear enough, but one further piece of writing fixed the doctrine of courtly love with absolute certainty. Eleanor's court at Poitiers broke up in 1174. The gallant participants returned to their own towns to practice the new principles as best they may. As a memorial to the days at Poitiers, and so that the true doctrine should not be lost, Marie of Champagne, on her return to Troyes, directed her chaplain to write a textbook for lovers. This was the *Art of Courtly Love* by Andreas Capellanus.

The work reveals Andreas as the type of worldly priest often found in the service of princes. In his opinion, the delicate and understanding clergy are supremely well suited for love, and though he ends his book with a perfunctory retraction, clearly he knew just what Marie meant by courtly love. The love they had in mind, though it had elements of disinterest and spirituality about it, was tormented, obsessive and definitely carnal: 'Love', Andreas wrote, 'is a certain inborn suffering derived from the sight of and excessive meditation upon the beauty of the opposite sex, which causes each one to wish above all things the embraces of the other and by common desire to carry out all of love's precepts in the embrace of the other.'

At the heart of courtly doctrine, as Andreas insists, was the conviction that love is the most civilizing force in society, 'the fountain and origin of all good things'. Everything that marks gentle society from barbarism springs from it: 'It is agreed among all men that there is no good thing in the world, and no courtesy, which is not derived from love.' A knight properly infatuated is generous, kind, mild, brave, gallant, and religious. The development of this bright claim leads Andreas down thorny paths of equivocation and contradiction.

To begin with, the beneficent effect of love can work only on knights and nobles, a prerogative of their class. Though peasants

The lovers, carving from the Maison d'Adam in Angers, France.

occasionally feel the itch of Venus 'like any horse or mule', hard labour and the 'uninterrupted solace of plough and mattock' should keep them in hand; they are not to be instructed in the theory of love lest they become diverted from useful toil. A knight unlucky enough to love a peasant girl should lead her to a quiet place and without more ado take her 'by force'. Next, courtly love cannot exist between married partners: marriage may lead to friendship, amiability, companionship, but never to love. Love must be granted freely and this (in the opinion of Countess Marie) is not so in marriage where two people 'are in duty bound to grant each other's desires and deny nothing'. Furthermore, 'jealousy', the spur and necessity of love, is avoided in marriage as a nuisance, 'but lovers should always welcome it as the mother and nurse of love'. On the cult of adultery the authorities are most firm. In the curious caselore from the 'courts of love' that Andreas appended to his book, the decisions of the great ladies who judge the causes universally condemn married love. As Queen Adèle, wife of Louis of France, puts it: 'We dare not oppose the Countess of Champagne, who ruled that love can exert no power between husband and wife.'

A benefit to Christian society so class-ridden and immoral is queer enough; that it should also appear frankly irreligious is more surprising, especially in a book written by a chaplain. Andreas exempted nuns from love's darts (but not priests, who were merely men and 'conceived in sin'); and he banned from courtly service those knights tainted with heresy or incest. But in an effort to proclaim the worthiness and benevolence of love, courtly devotion is made to appear the passport to salvation. In an attractive and lively allegory, Andreas depicts a knight taken to the land of the dead where he sees first the country of Delight, inhabited by those fair women who served love well on earth and in reward are gallantly serviced by the God of Love 'in a marvellous fashion' each according to her deserts; next he sees the boggy country of Humidity given over to those 'shameless women' who followed pleasure but not courtesy, who 'assented to the lust of any man that asked them'; and finally he sees the wretched women in the hell of Aridity, suffering among thorns for their chastity, who 'closed the palace of Love to all who wished to enter it'. Poor logic and bad analogy indicate what Andreas perhaps dimly perceived: that the fully developed theory of *Frauendienst*—the worshipful service of women—was highly un-Christian and not supportable without some intellectual sleight-of-hand.

The code of courtly love was more commended than practised. The clamorous voices of the Church naturally shouted against it, and those that tried to act on it sometimes ran into a primitive and most uncourtly violence. It is said that the devotion of the knight Walter de Fontaines for Countess Isabelle of Flanders aroused the anger of her husband. In 1175 he had his wife disgraced and her lover killed in a most shameful manner.

But the theory was attractive to knights, for it confirmed their superiority and difference to the rest of society, since even their love

The knight as the saviour and protector of ladies. Early sculpture from the Cathedral of Angoulême.

was of a rare and subtle breed. And it was attractive to poets since it gave them the vast, new region of the human heart to explore in poems that were guaranteed to please the courtly audience they wrote for. Troubadours of the south, trouvères of France and of the French-speaking English court, minnesingers of Germany, poets of the *dolce stil nuovo* in Italy, all celebrated the ideal of courtly love. Out of this varying and inconsistent body of courtly poetry came a new and astonishing emotion to afflict the western heart, the feeling of romantic passion. Romance was seen as a courteous display, an exaggerated game of hope and despair; passion was seen as an irresistible sexual drive, something imperious, freely given, all demanding, outside morality. Joined together they gave a sudden and startling lift to the chivalrous knight's apprehension of the world. He was overcome by subtleties of joy and surprise perceived through love, and most appropriately expressed by love's good servant Bernart de Ventadorn:

My heart is full of joy
    and all seems changed:
Winter's cold transformed to flowers
    white, and red, and yellow.
With the wind and the rain
    my joy increases,
My merit mounts and rises,
    and my song grows good.
Such love lies in my heart,
    such joy and sweetness,
The ice seems like flowers,
    and the snow green fields.

The knight of chivalry had become, in that phrase which Edward Gibbon blushed to express, 'the champion of God and the ladies'.

# chapter five

Did he ever exist, this knight of faith and courtesy? At the beginning of the twelfth century, century of crusaders and troubadours, Guibert de Nogent looked hard and could not find him. 'The order of knighthood', wrote Peter of Blois some fifty years later, 'is nowadays mere disorder.' By the end of the century Chrétien de Troyes, arch-poet of romance, had pronounced the obsequies. 'The age of chivalry', he wrote in *Yvain*, 'is dead.' Complexities of the world betrayed that idealism, poor child of innocent illusion.

The crusades, the first chivalrous enterprise, promised unusual advantages to knights, and they leapt into the business with a thoughtless enthusiasm that guaranteed an early fall. Profit, honour, even salvation seemed within the reach of the most loutish brigand; and best of all, a warrior could assume virtue without any inconvenient change of habit. An amiable Church (or so it appeared) had

Departure of the Crusaders, from a 12th Cent fresco at Cressac, France.

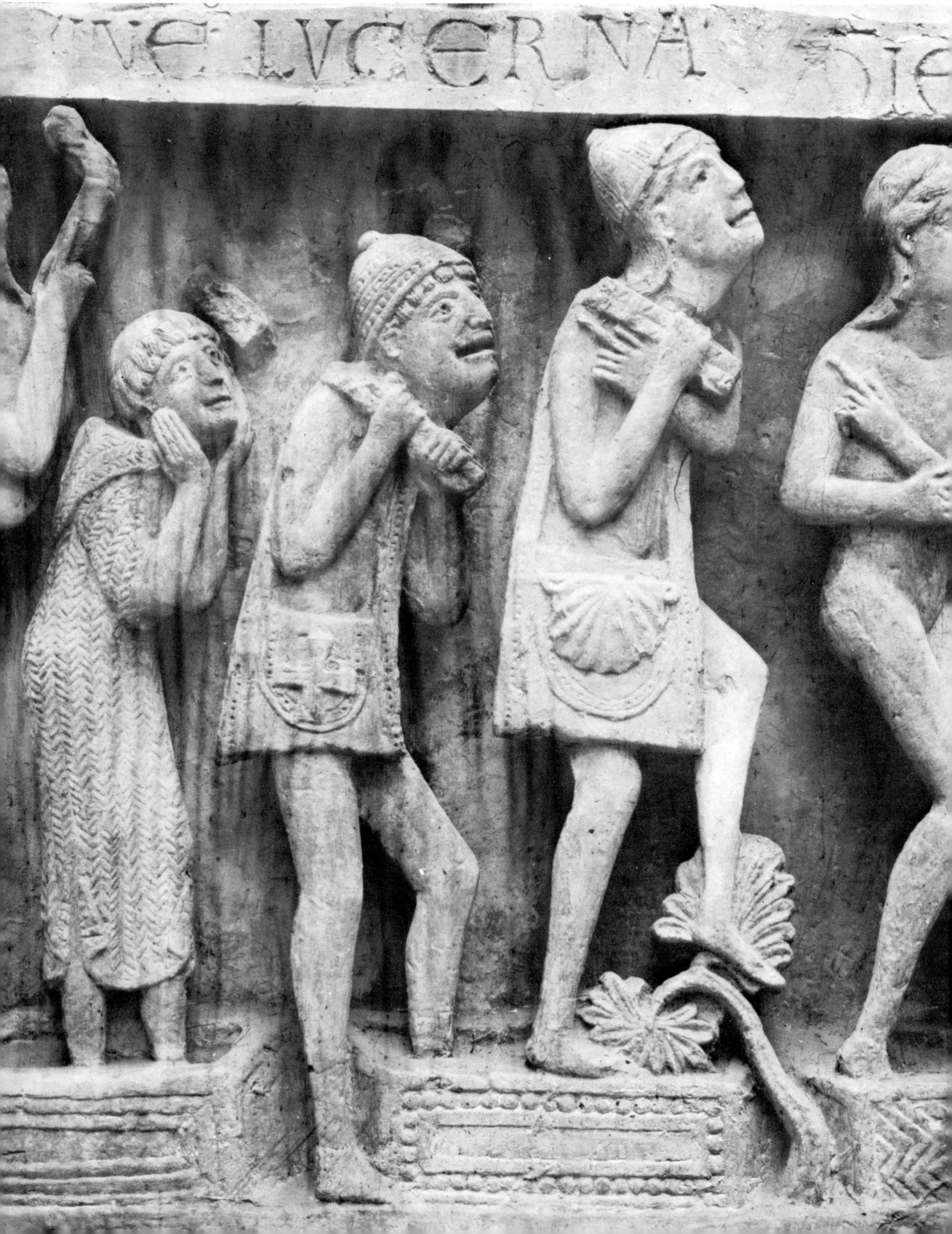
LVCERNA

consecrated the life of warfare so dear to the rugged feudal heart that 'loved battle', said the *Chanson d'Antioche*, 'better than money or fine gold'.

'If I had one foot in heaven and the other on the edge of battle,' cried a character in *Garin li Loherains*, 'I would withdraw the foot from heaven and go to the fight.' Providentially, the chivalrous crusader could expect both the glory of the battle and the solace of heaven. And he had certain terrestrial benefits as well; for having once taken the cross of the crusader a knight was protected by the *privilegium crucis*, the 'privilege of the cross' that preserved him from the ordinary operation of the law: his debts could mount, his enemies could prosecute in vain. The knight committed to a crusade was a man outside the normal order, loose among the shoals of delusion. Cynical men worked the privilege of the cross for their own ends. The larger number of knights with a true chivalrous intent made a confession of their sins and a reparation of their wrongs, bought Masses for their souls, endowed abbeys and churches, sometimes enfranchised their villeins, often sold up their estates, and in a kind of holy intemperance, fortified in soul but in deepest ignorance and considerable poverty, hurried away to meet the unknown trials and great expense of a crusade. The experience of the Holy Land was a stiff re-education in the nature of reality.

How hard it was, amid muddle and ignorance, to keep the ideal. Almost the first act of the First Crusade was a surprising denial of good faith. Pope Urban's call was taken up immediately by the People's Crusade, the army of the poor incited by such famous preachers as Peter the Hermit, led more by dreams than by sense, and in such disarray that the peasant crusaders hardly knew their fellows let alone their destination. Strangers arrived from goodness knows what unspeakable nations (wrote Guibert de Nogent) claiming to owe God the same allegiance as did the Franks, marching hopefully with shaggy hair, bare legs, clothed in skins, bearing eager expectations, villainous weapons and meagre supplies. There were some, wrote Guibert, 'who spoke such gibberish that, unable to make themselves understood, they put their fingers in the form of a cross, to show by signs, lacking words, that they wanted to serve in the cause of faith'.

In haste to be at an enemy whom none had seen, few could place and fewer recognise, the rabble got away well before the proper crusade of the nobles. In Germany, a sly robber-baron directed their ignorant fury against prosperous Jewish communities. In Hungary, the pack began to maul the countryside, and 'forgetting the hospitality and benevolence of the Hungarians, made war on them for no reason', burning granaries, raping women, robbing all comers. By August 1096 the dangerous mob was at Constantinople where it behaved, wrote Anna Comnena, 'with the utmost insolence, pulling down palaces, setting fire to buildings, stripping lead from church roofs and selling it to the Greeks'. The Greek Emperor, Anna's father, hustled the peasants over the Bosphorus; without sense or discipline they came abruptly against the Turkish horsemen who trapped them on the frontier. 'Our men', said the *Gesta*

Medieval pilgrimage: the traveller to the Holy Land, on the left, wears the cross on his wallet; the pilgrim to the famous shrine of St James of Compostela, on the right, wears the scallop shell on his wallet. A 12th Cent carving from Autun.

*Francorum*, noting the stark awakening from the stupid frolic, 'suffered so much from thirst that they opened the veins of horses and donkeys to drink the blood; some dipped rags in latrines and squeezed the slime of excrement into their mouths; others urinated into the hands of a companion and then drank.' Those who escaped this siege were caught at Civetot and massacred, leaving behind a vast pile of bones which later crusaders (wrote Anna Comnena) used to repair the walls, 'and thus made of that city as it were their tomb'.

The warning of the People's Crusade made no impression on the following knights. A business that needed the greatest sagacity, planning and sound leadership went forward with presumption, disorder and jealous squabbles. Only bravery and an almost superhuman endurance saw the knights through to the Holy Land. Such is often the way of idealism. A traditional fear of the sea and an ignorance of geography led the crusaders into extraordinary land routes, wandering amazed in mountains and dry rocks, set on by angry tribes, encumbered with useless baggage, but short of food and always thirsty. In a feudal army of several nations, without the clear ties of lord and vassal, each leader thought himself the equal of the next noble, and did not hesitate to exercise a capricious and selfish judgment. None of the great princes, neither Raymond of Saint-Gilles nor Robert of Flanders nor Stephen of Blois nor Hugh of Vermandois, could establish an ascendancy, and their deliberations, more or less well-intentioned, were always bedevilled by the presence of Bohemond of Taranto, the Norman desperado whose brutality and self-interest made him the type of many later crusaders. A well-tried mercenary who knew something of the Saracens and had fought the Byzantines, Bohemond was the professional who guided the innocents, much to their confusion. Anna Comnena put her appreciative eye over his fine form—his clear white skin, ruddy cheeks, short red hair, blue eyes, mighty shoulders—but admitted to tingling of apprehension whenever his loud, treacherous laughter was heard: 'This warrior had a certain charm, somewhat spoiled, however, by the feeling of terror that he inspired.'

Led on by Frankish simplicity and Norman cunning the crusaders first met the Turks in June 1097, at Nicaea, and repulsed them. A month later the western knights gained another lucky victory at Dorylaeum. Turning towards Antioch, into the heart of Moslem territory, the Christian army, fortified by two encounters, seemed brave enough for any romance of chivalry. 'The crusaders', wrote Albert of Aix, 'in all the splendour of their shields of gold, green, red and various other colours, unfurling banners of gold and purple, marched towards Antioch, mounted on great horses, bearing glittering helms and bucklers.' That bravery covered the fresh scars of experience. Ignorance of Turkish tactics and the usual careless misunderstanding between the leaders made the victory at Dorylaeum an unnecessary close thing. The march after the Turks into Syria was more a weary penance than a triumphant progress. 'We pursued them', said the *Gesta*, 'across deserts and an uninhabitable land without water which we scarcely came through alive.' After thirst and fatigue by day and the bitter cold of the desert by night, Fulcher of

The journey from London to Jerusalem, set out by the St Albans chronicler Matthew Paris about 1250, with representations of important towns and the length of each day's journey. (*Continued overleaf*)

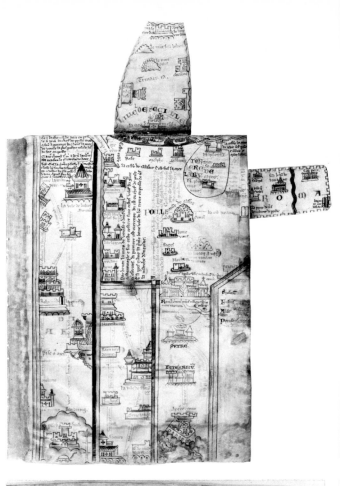

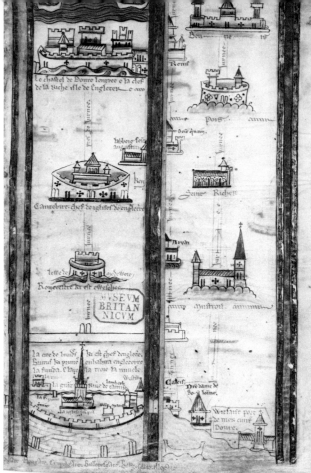

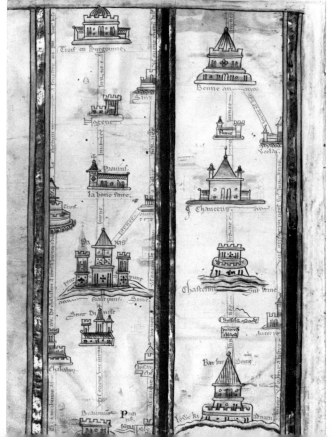

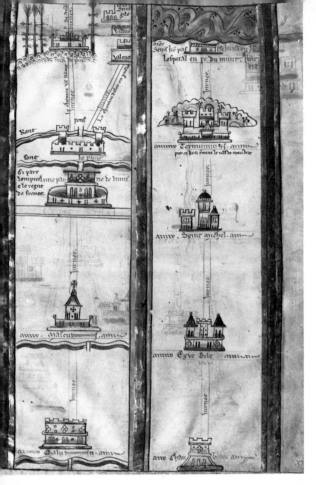

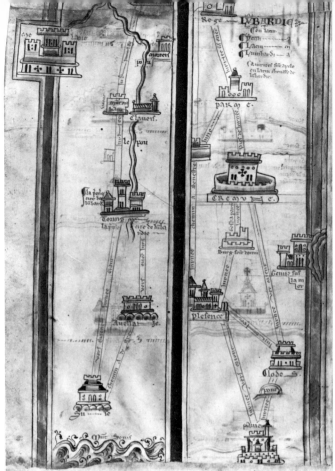

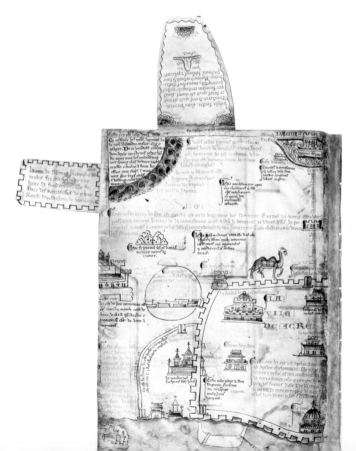

Chartres mentioned the added danger of flash storms: 'I saw many of our people perish from these cold rains, for lack of tents to shelter in.' From the desert the crusaders entered the mountains where trials increased. 'The horses fell headlong into the ravines, one pack animal dragging down another. On every side the knights gave way to despair and beat their breasts for sorrow and sadness, cursing themselves and their arms. They sold their shields, their good coats of mail, their helmets and equipment for five deniers or less. Those who could find no buyer threw their stuff by the road and went on.' An army in an ugly mood sat down before Antioch, where the Moslems kept the crusaders at bay for nearly a year. Physical distress, disappointment and the frustrations of delay put chivalrous conduct to flight. A destitute soldiery, on the verge of famine, began to forage and pillage. To terrify the enemy into submission, Bohemond had captives killed and roasted as if for a cannibal feast. Yet when Antioch fell, in June 1098, it was only through the treachery of a Moslem, and then the crusaders were in their turn blockaded by the Emir Kerbuqa, subjected once more to starvation, eating dead donkeys, paying a gold bezant for a scrap of bread, two sous for an egg, a denier for a nut. Rich and poor deserted. One of the chief barons, Stephen of Blois, got clean away; but Peter the Hermit, wretched survivor of the peasant army and still a talisman for the crusade, was dragged back by the brawny arm of Bohemond himself.

Spurred on by a desperate shame, and by the supposed discovery of the Holy Lance, the Christians at last drove out of Antioch. And the intoxication of blood first tasted in that city, which they had

*Below*. The siege of Antioch during the First Crusade. The artist shows the light weapons and armour of the Saracen, while the Western cavalry is in full heavy armour and armed with the usual lance. The actual attack on the walls seems to be undertaken by foot-soldiers armed with axe or crossbow and, in some cases, without armour. From a 14th Cent manuscript.

*Overleaf*. The hills near Jerusalem through which the First Crusaders advanced in the summer heat.

taken with such thoroughgoing slaughter that the streets were impassable for stinking corpses, carried them on a tide of gore towards Jerusalem. 'At Ma'arrat an-Nu'man', wrote the historian ibn al-Athir, 'for three days the slaughter never stopped.' A kind of frenzy, part bloodlust part religious hysteria, seemed to possess the crusaders as they approached the Holy City. Individual knights broke away in wild rushes just to glimpse the walls. It was June, hot and excessively dry. Chroniclers spoke of a feeling of suffocation, of lassitude interspersed with bouts of daemonic energy. The walls were invested, towers and siege-engines prepared. When all was ready, the crusaders walked in procession beneath the ramparts, fasting and praying. On 14th July 1099 the siege-towers were in place and the assault began. After a day of hectic struggle a breach was made and about midday on the fifteenth the knight Litold of Tournai gained the first foothold on the walls. 'As soon as he reached the top', the *Gesta* recorded, 'all the defenders of the town fled through the city and our men followed them and harried them, felling and killing them right up to the Temple of Solomon, where there was such a carnage that our men were wading in Saracen blood up to their ankles.' Ibn al-Athir gave the Moslem view of the shambles, the population put to the sword, the Dome of the Rock looted, and the city pillaged for a week: 'In the Masjid al-Aqsa the Franks killed more than seventy thousand people, among them a large number of imams and scholars, devout and ascetic men, far from their homelands, living in the pious seclusion of the Holy Places.'

That holy work, the taking of Jerusalem, was the justification of military chivalry. What did the commentators make of the triumphant moment? William of Tyre shrank from the monstrous victors 'covered head to foot in blood'. The sword cut and plunged until an exhaustion of satiety stopped it, leaving the city a charnel-house. 'Orders were given at least', said the *Gesta*, 'that all the dead Saracens should be thrown beyond the walls because of the terrible stench, for the whole city was almost entirely filled with corpses. The living Saracens dragged the dead out of the town and made piles of them almost as high as the houses. No one had ever seen, no one had even heard of such a carnage among the pagan race. Funeral pyres were set up like milestones, and none but God knows their number.'

When Jerusalem was conquered a great number of the crusaders immediately set out for home: the task of chivalry was done. Within a week a large party of Egyptian troops rallied to attack the city, and Godfrey of Bouillon, the newly elected ruler, had to send in haste to the departing knights to turn about and continue the battle. The appalling light of a sudden illumination afflicted the western knights. To be a soldier of Christ, to be a truly chivalrous warrior, was not, as so many rashly thought, the gallant work of a moment, but the hard labour of a lifetime.

For nearly two hundred years chivalry struggled to express itself through the great pilgrimage to the Holy Land and through the guardianship of the Holy Places. Streams of exhortation and propaganda nourished the frail shoots of noble idealism. The powerful

*Top*. The walls of the citadel of Jerusalem, with the Tower of David.

*Above*. Fulk de Neuilly, one of the chief papal agents for promoting the Crusades, preaching in France in 1198. From the *Conquest of Constantinople* by Villehardouin.

rhetoric of Peter the Hermit was not exceptional. The lash of stinging sermons beat continually on penitent shoulders. When St Bernard preached the Second Crusade at Vézelay, so many came forward that he quickly ran out of the cloth crosses which crusaders wore, and he tore his own garments into strips to accommodate the crowd. Fulk de Neuilly, a chief agent of Innocent III for promoting crusading zeal, 'struck the hearts of wicked men like arrows and brought them to tears and repentance'. Fulk was chosen by God, exclaimed Jacques de Vitry, 'to be a rain in time of drought so that His vine may be tended'. De Vitry himself, a famous preacher and at one time Bishop of Acre, could so move a crowd that idlers and miscreants in thousands clamoured to take the cross. He proved this at Genoa in 1216, though he modestly admitted that he did not even know the language.

And the plain speaking of the preacher was supported by the more subtle propaganda of the poet. From the time of the *Chanson de Roland*, the epic of pilgrimage was the great theme of Christian poetry. And Christian deeds in the Holy Land, real or fabulous, soon became themselves the stuff of legend, the inspiration for such works as the *Chanson d'Antioche* and the *Chanson de Jerusalem*. The troubadours, men of doubtful virtue that they were, knew well the imaginative appeal of the crusading message. Too often reluctant to make the journey themselves, they recommended it to others as a chivalrous and noble duty. In a fine, appropriate phrase Marcabrun called the land of crusade 'our virtuous cleansing place' where sins of knighthood are washed away. Giraut de Borneil wrote poems to remind Richard Lionheart of his crusading vow.

With such encouragement, there were always some pious chevaliers to make the pilgrimage with true devotion and defend the Holy Places, men with poignant dreams uncorrupted by a bad awakening. Raymond of Saint-Gilles, richest and most powerful leader of the First Crusade, left the slaughter at Ma'arrat an-Nu'man barefoot and in sackcloth, to remind his fellow Christians that there was more to a crusade than the murder of Moslems and the collection of booty. Godfrey of Bouillon, chosen ruler of Jerusalem, refused the title of king because he would not wear a crown of gold where his Saviour had worn a crown of thorns. From Louis VII to his descendant St Louis IX a hundred years later, the chroniclers had always some tale to tell of Christian mercy, generosity, courage or faith, a tale of those who emulated Raymond or Godfrey, a lesson in true chivalry.

But for most, the dream so assiduously peddled in Europe began to dissolve with the first rays of the hard eastern light. It is no wonder that the troubadour William of Poitiers grew to hate the crusade; his journey in 1101 seemed an epitome of suffering. One of his colleagues, with a grandiose stupidity, led a large part of the army well into Persia where the slow-moving westerners were cut down at leisure by the light marauding horsemen of the enemy. William himself, with the men of Aquitaine, took a more sensible route, but failed (as happened too often) to look to the water-supply. Having crossed the desert to Heraclea, the army broke ranks in a

Pillar of the Church of the Holy Sepulchre in Jerusalem, covered with the marks of the Crusaders.

parched delirium to reach the river, where they were easily cut off and killed by the Turks. Of a grand force said to number some two hundred thousand, less than ten thousand struggled through to Antioch.

An ordinary crusader had his fill of misfortune and suffering before ever he reached the Holy Land. The Emperor Conrad, in the Second Crusade, having neglected to bring cross-bow men was so mercilessly harried by flying columns that he was forced to turn back and retreat in disarray to the Bosphorus; thirty thousand of his men, said Odo de Deuil, died of exposure, exhaustion and dysentery, besides those killed by the enemy. His co-leader, Louis VII, took a more cautious route and was going well until the casual incompetence of his vanguard let the French into an ambush. In the mêlée

Conrad III, wearing the two-headed eagle of the German Emperor, and Louis VII, bearing the fleur-de-lis of France, fight together against the Saracen on their ill-fated Second Crusade. From the *Chronique de St Denis*.

Louis fought alone, with his back to a rock, and owed his life to his sword-play. Baggage and stores, thousands of horses, great numbers of pilgrims and many knights were lost that day. Not even the great experience and outstanding generalship of Emperor Frederick Barbarossa could bring the German army of the Third Crusade safely through Turkey. Barbarossa easily beat the Turks at each encounter, but the familiar evils of sickness, hunger and thirst, and lack of forage made skeletons of men and horses. Barbarossa himself was accidentally drowned in the waters of the Calycadnus on 10th June 1190, and his leaderless troops just made it to Antioch 'after six weeks of marching and starving'.

A hundred years of ruinous misadventure finally persuaded the western knight to overcome his fear of the sea. Later crusaders who

*Below.* Two ways to the Holy Land: *left*, the land route, harrassed by flying columns of Saracens; *right*, the uncomfortable sea-journey in small ships. From the *Secreta fidelium crucis*, 1321.

*Right.* The capture of Damietta, at the mouth of the Nile, by St Louis in the summer of 1249. This early Christian success was followed by failure; not long after St Louis himself was captured at the disastrous Christian defeat at Mansura.

travelled to the Holy Land by ship, despite the discomfort and fearsome stench of men and animals tumbling together in a bucking hold, at least had a likelihood of reaching the destination. But by then military chivalry had a sour taste. The battle merely to subsist was a greater preoccupation than the holy war against the infidel. Hunger, thirst, exposure and sickness, the unnecessary pains caused by bad planning, bad judgment and bad luck, were the constant theme of western memoirs. William of Tyre tells of the noble ladies with the First Crusade who starved in the houses of Antioch rather than go out and be seen to beg, and of the knights who prowled the streets sniffing for food which they would snatch uninvited. In the many chronicles, the calamity of dryness, leading inevitably to debilitation and perhaps death from thirst, malnutrition, heatstroke, diphtheria and dysentery, was monotonously followed by the calamity of the downpour, leading inevitably to debilitation and perhaps death from cold, exposure, malaria and typhoid. The expedition of St Louis found that some hundred and fifty years of fighting in the east had done very little to teach wisdom to the crusader. 'During the whole of Lent', wrote Joinville from the Delta of the Nile, 'we ate no fish except eels; and the eels, which are ravenous feeders, fed on corpses. This wretched diet and the unhealthy country where no rain falls brought upon us the camp fever which caused the flesh of the legs to dry up and the skin to be covered with black and brown spots, just like an old boot. And when we caught the disease the flesh of our gums began to drop away. Nobody recovered from it.' To observe the Church rules for Lent, in the teeth of the enemy and in an unforgiving land, the crusaders ate eels gorged on contaminated corpses, sickened and died. Acts of idealistic simplicity, common on every crusade, were very close to suicide. In the same unworldly spirit Joinville once thrust away a dish of much-needed meat when he was reminded that the day was Friday.

Since crusaders set out in a wilful darkness, their actual experience in the east was likely to be a puzzle or a revelation, which in either case questioned the chivalric assumptions of Europe. Knowledge of Arab or Turk was alarmingly defective. There was one opinion that the 'Saracen' (the undifferentiated Moslem) was a secret kinsman of the Frank, a knight in all respects except for his unfortunate faith. There was another opinion that confused the Saracen with the Jew, and would attack him with impunity anywhere in the world as one of a race that had crucified Christ. A Moslem chief, given this reason for an unwarranted attack by Christians, had to correct the theological history of his aggressors. Nor were the crusaders ready to take advice. The Greeks of the Byzantine Empire knew the Moslem well, in war and peace; but crusader and Greek disliked each other, and the westerners preferred to follow their misconceptions into disaster.

Too much knowledge was a danger. A knight engaged in the weary campaigns against the infidel would rather look on his adversary as a treacherous, cruel barbarian whom a just man would rightly abominate. But close mixing with the Moslem usually calmed the

The Holy City of Jerusalem seen on the distant mountain-top.

leg, one doctor prescribed a strong man with an axe; the leg was put on a block, the axe swung, and the knight died instantly of shock. For another poor woman with consumption, the doctor cunningly diagnosed a devil in the head, trepanned the skull, rubbed salt in the wound, and again killed the patient. And the Arabs could teach a lesson in much besides medicine. Nearly every Moslem town had wonders to display. Travellers noted the well-watered fertility of northern Syria, small towns set like jewels in the midst of orchards and gardens. Tripoli was a thousand cubits long and as many wide, its houses four, five and sometimes six storeys high, dwellings and bazaars so clean they could pass for palaces. Aleppo had vast bazaars, all roofed and shaded, the chief one 'like an enclosed garden, so gracious and beautiful it is'. And as for Cairo, a chronicler relates the amazement of two knights at the riches they saw there, 'fountains of marble filled with sparkling water over which flocks of birds unknown to us fluttered and sang. Galleries were lined with marble columns, sheathed with gold and covered with carvings. The floors were a mosaic of delicate material'. The evidence of trade, culture and luxury was overwhelming.

And the Moslem himself, with the possible exception of the most primitive of the Turkish tribesmen, was a man that a soldier could respect and even like. The fatalism of Islam often made the enemy atrociously cruel, sometimes (as was the case with Saladin against the Templars) in retaliation for crusader offences; but the Saracen was just as likely to be brave, magnanimous and merciful. The acts of chivalry were by no means on one side only, and the chronicles abound with honourable episodes of Moslem gallantry and clemency. The finer qualities of the adversary were seen as early as the First Crusade. 'Who is wise and learned enough to describe the sagacity, energy and valour of the Saracen?' wrote the author of the *Gesta*. 'In truth, had they but kept the faith of Christ, none could have equalled them in power, courage and the arts of war.'

The mingling of Christian and Moslem in the long years of the Latin occupation modified the simple ardour of the crusader's fierce heart. A mutual respect led to peaceful co-existence. In the kingdom of Syria, in the century between the Third Crusade and the final expulsion of the knights, there were no less than eighty years of peace. The Christian long resident in the east was more a colonist than a defender of the faith, more interested in scythe and shears than sword and lance, and he soon became a bit of an Oriental himself. 'We have already forgotten the places where we were born,' wrote the chronicler Fulcher in 1120. 'Some already possess houses and servants as a hereditary right. Some have taken foreign wives, Syrian, Armenian, even baptised Saracen women; others have a house full of alien in-laws; one cultivates his vines, another his fields; they speak many languages, but understand each other.' Apostasy and conversion according to convenience went on among both peoples, to the scandal of both Christian and Moslem. Usama regretted the presence of Franks 'who have settled in our land and live like Moslems', but found these 'better than the ones just arrived from their homelands'. Certainly, they were better from the Moslem point of view;

*Below*. Siege warfare of the Crusades. Since the command of the prosperous cities of the Levant was the key to possession of the Holy Land, Crusaders were forced to spend much time attacking or defending walled cities. From the narration of the Crusades in the *Grand Conquest Beyond the Seas* of the 12th Cent.

*Right*. Arab cavalry, from a Persian miniature of the 16th Cent.

*Opposite*. The effigy of the Crusader Sir John Holcombe who died of wounds during the Second Crusade. Dorchester Abbey, *c.* 1270.

*Opposite, below*. The Eastern view of Moslem warfare against Christians. A Moslem assault on a fortress of the Knights of St John. From the Persian manuscript known as the Garrett Zafar-nama, 1467.

the newcomers arrived full of uncompromising crusading zeal, ready to make the infidel jump; the settlers had no thought of further conquest, being anxious for a quiet life.

Ignorant of geography and eastern history, the crusaders were especially ignorant of the political consequences of their action. They came forward pell-mell, unthinkingly, and this incursion of soldiers who blended worldly naïvety with raw strength in a most dangerous way was very alarming to anyone with a traditional interest in the eastern Mediterranean lands. The Greek emperors watched the crusaders cross their domain with well-justified apprehension, and directed against them the famous wiles of Byzantine policy. There was bad blood on both sides. Hostility was kept in bounds for a century but at last burst out with the events of the Fourth Crusade, the crusade that never reached Jerusalem but turned aside, and spurred on by the Venetians, besieged, sacked and occupied Constantinople in 1204.

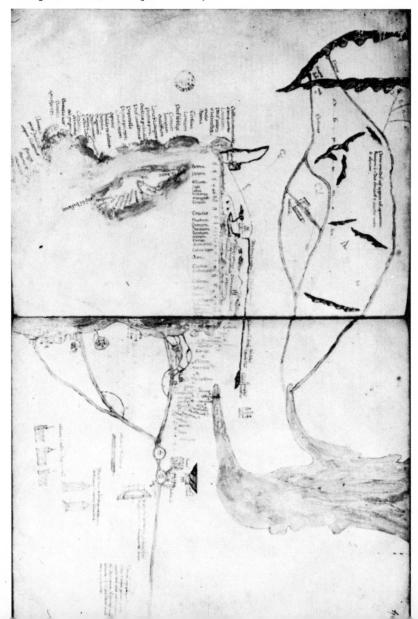

Medieval map of the Middle East showing Babylon, Mecca, Antioch, Cairo and Jerusalem, and also showing the irrigation of the Nile Valley and the presence of abbeys in the Egyptian desert. From the *Secreta fidelium crucis*, the Italian handbook for Crusaders composed in Venice in 1321.

The problem of the Byzantines was resolved in a traditional way with a display of brute force. The invasion of the Holy Land caused problems that were not so easily solved. After it was clear that the knights would have to stay to preserve the freedom of the Holy Places, there was the puzzling question of how the Christian forces were to be organized. Churchmen naturally wanted the city of Christ, won in a holy crusade, to be ruled by the Church. But the constant danger from the Saracens made a military rule necessary, and in a muddle of haste the great barons imitated the only kind of polity they knew: they devised a feudal principality to be governed, according to true chivalry, not by the most important baron (who was Raymond of Saint-Gilles), nor by the best soldier (who was Bohemond), but by the most holy knight Godfrey of Bouillon.

It was fitting that military aristocrats, archetypal feudal men, should set up the feudal state in its purest form, demonstrating only too well all the drawbacks of feudalism. The eastern lands, as they were conquered, were split up into small feudal kingdoms, fragmented, capricious, independent, family concerns bound by individual ties of loyalty with less interest in the common cause. The family of Godfrey, who soon died, received the kingdom of Jerusalem, and Judaea was parcelled out among his vassals. The principality of Edessa went to Godfrey's cousin, Baldwin of Le Bourg. Bohemond got his unclean hands on the principality of Antioch. After the capture of Tripoli in 1109, the family of Raymond was rewarded with this county. Each little kingdom was a separate

mons aurrus

onadri vero sci martin
Turonensis hoc tempore vivebant nimis deliciose et
induebantur vestibus sericis eorumqꝛ calciamenta

A medieval ship such as those used by the Italian city-states for commerce and for the transport of Crusaders to the Holy Land. Mosaic in Ravenna, *c.* 1213.

entity, weak because of few numbers, lack of supplies and reinforcements. The Christians clustered round the coast where they could rely on the support of the Italian city-states with their strong navies. Between the kingdoms, eternally threatening them, and stretching to the interior of Syria were the bold ranks of Saracens. The crusading dynasties were at first resourceful and energetic, great builders, active marauders, surprisingly successful administrators and traders. At the furthest extent of their conquests, before Zangi pulled together the disorganized enemy in 1129, things looked black for the Moslems. Westerners prowled from Mesopotamia to the Mediterranean, from Turkey to the Egyptian border. The whole land was infested with plundering knights, wrote the historian of Zangi's reign: 'Merchants and travellers had to hide among the rocks, or trust themselves and their goods to the mercy of the Bedouin. Things were going worse and worse, and the Christians had begun to blackmail the surviving Moslem towns, which paid to be quit of their terrible devastations. They took a regular tribute from all the territory of Aleppo as far as the mill outside the garden gate, only twenty paces from the city itself.'

But that was only one side of the story. Moslems living under Christian rule were not oppressed; indeed they often paid fewer

The Krak des Chevaliers, in Syria, one of the massive, strategic castles that the Crusaders established in the Holy Land.

dues than Christian settlers, being free from the ecclesiastical tithe. A Spanish Moslem, passing through Syria on the return from Mecca in 1184, testified to the prosperity of the subject race: 'We left Toron by a road lined throughout with Moslem farms, existing in great prosperity under the Franks (may God preserve us from a similar temptation!). They give their masters half their crop, pay a poll-tax, and a light tax on fruit trees. But the Moslems are masters in their own houses and order their affairs as they like. Such is the constitution of their farms and villages in Frankish territory. Many Moslems long in their hearts to settle there, knowing the misery of their brethren in districts under Moslem rule.'

The occupation of the Holy Land was no triumphant onrush of chivalrous endeavour, an implacable advance of Christian peoples united in holy purpose against an infidel presence, but rather a broken pattern of ordinary military invasion and settlement, leading to feudal principalities with familiar features, good and bad, inherently weak from internal jealousies and divisions, veering about to the winds of war and trade, existing as best they may. The holy struggle against the Saracens went by fits and starts, only going forward with any sense of devotion when from time to time an exceptional leader managed to rally the bickering feudal chiefs to

A street of shops in the late Middle Ages, which saw the flourishing growth of towns and the rise of the merchant and the bourgeois as persons of commercial and political power. From a 15th Cent manuscript.

The contests of chivalry: the clash
of knights resplendent in their
heraldic devices. From French
Gothic painting of the 14th Cent.

One of the oldest known portraits of the French king and famous Crusader, Saint Louis IX. From an early 14th Cent manuscript.

the tattered banner of Christendom. This did not happen often. Baldwin IV, the tragic leper-King of Jerusalem, though only a lad in his teens and ravaged by his dreadful disease, heroically resisted the might of Saladin, winning the famous victory of Montgisard in 1177, five hundred knights, eighty Templars and some two thousand foot-soldiers routing 30,000 mamluks commanded by Saladin himself. After Baldwin died from his disease at the age of twenty-four, the powerful figure of Conrad of Montferrat pressed for the

Third Crusade, arranging it almost single-handed if we believe the historian Baha ad-Din, who related that Conrad, to rouse the princes of Europe, had a picture painted and universally displayed in which a Moslem horseman trampled Christ's tomb while his horse urinated on it. The Saracens were glad to see the murder of Conrad at Tyre in 1192, by some accounts killed on the orders of Richard Lionheart and by other accounts executed by the Assassins. Apart from Conrad, the chief military dangers to Islam came from the unbalanced enthusiasm of Richard Lionheart and, fifty years later, from the gallant impetuosity of St Louis, in justice, mercy and piety the perfect crusader, but an unwary campaigner and ineffective general.

For most knights, whether newcoming crusaders off the latest ship or old restraints long burnt by the eastern sun, the Holy Land was merely an adventure ground where feudal soldiers could follow their usual diversions, seeking excitement, fame and riches. The rogues outnumbered the chevaliers, and were, on the whole, more effective. The Christian armies were better directed by the un-principled Bohemond or the violent Richard Lionheart, than by the pious Godfrey or St Louis. The greatest political success of the crusades was won by that excommunicated prince of duplicity, the Emperor Frederick II, who in 1228 temporarily repossessed Jerusalem by negotiation, without striking a blow and without even (as his enemies alleged and his friends suspected) believing in God.

The First Crusade was disrupted by the quarrels of the barons. Later crusades were torn by the greater egotism of monarchs. On the Second Crusade the antipathy between Conrad and his Germans and Louis and his Frenchmen caused many bloody incidents. 'Our own men', wrote Odo de Deuil with fine French prejudice, 'could not bear those Germans.' Philip Augustus of France and Richard Lionheart of England were determined competitors on the Third Crusade, each trying to outdo the other in all the graces of kingship. Philip promised his knights three gold bezants a month; Richard raised his offer to four bezants. Any act of gallantry that Philip performed, Richard could outbrave with an act yet more reckless and impressive. At last, the astute French king declared it no contest and went home, to the shame of French chivalry. 'The barons of France', wrote the Norman chronicler Ambroise, 'were full of fury and anger when they saw that their leader, whose vassals they were, was so decided that neither tears nor laments could make him agree to remain.' They came close to disowning their lord and their King.

If monarchs used the crusade for the furtherance of ambition, one could expect no less from their inferiors. The various barons who aspired to an eastern territory used any means to gain their end. Christians allied themselves to Moslems, either to fight Saracen or fellow baron, and in these plots the barons were helped by the fractious divisions between the Moslem princes who disliked each other as keenly as they disliked the Christians. The events leading up to the Christian disaster at the Battle of Hittin in 1187 were largely precipitated by the sullen disappointment of Raymond, Count of

*Left.* The Castle of Roquefixade. For the long campaigns of the Albigensian Crusade, Cathar resistance centred on strong, isolated castles, perched high in the hills of the Pyrenees, hard to reach and very difficult to attack. Over a period of thirty years they were reduced and demolished one by one.

*Below, left.* The Castle of Montsegur, remote and almost unreachable on its mountain-top, the last Cathar fortress to fall to the Albigensian Crusaders.

*Right.* The Crusader Reynald de Châtillon, a brutal and faithless opportunist, maltreats the Patriarch of Antioch, pouring honey on his head and locking him in a tower. From a 14th Cent manuscript.

Tripoli, who (wrote ibn al-Athir) went over to Saladin when he failed to get the kingship. 'Some Franks followed his example,' the Arab historian continued, 'which led to discord and disunity, and was one of the chief reasons why their towns were reconquered and Jerusalem fell to the Moslems.'

The promoters of 'discord and disunity' (perennial ground-bass to western woe) were often displaced, impecunious knights with a high-flying conceit who schemed for advancement in the east. Men like Guy of Lusignan, who by marriage and deception wormed his way to the kingship of Jerusalem in 1186, but alienated even the most callous by stupid cruelties, as when he massacred peaceful Bedouin shepherds in the region of Ascalon. Or men like Guy's lowly confederates, the two faithless opportunists Reynald of Châtillon and Gerard de Ridfort, Master of the Templars, whose sins caused the chivalrous and merciful Saladin to take a terrible vengeance. When Reynald broke a truce which Saladin had graciously conceded, the Moslem leader swore to kill him. Captured at Hittin, Reynald was brought before Saladin, who threw in the knight's teeth his broken vows and treaties, his manifest treacheries, and then struck him down saying, 'This man's evil deeds have caused his downfall, and you see here the wages of perfidy'. As for the military orders of Templars and Hospitallers, they had so incensed Saladin that he committed on them the most grisly act of his generally honourable career. After Hittin, vowing 'to purify the land of these impure races', he took a hundred or so and had them executed in his

Saladin seen through Western eyes. In this illustration the Saracen chief orders the chaining of Christian captives.

presence, many of the avenging swords being wielded by ascetics and sufis who clamoured for the right to kill their opponents.

While baron and adventurer perjured, schemed and murdered for their gains, the ordinary knight of the cavalry and the foot-soldier of the despised infantry registered their dismay and weariness, their indifference to idealism, in the usual way of the ranks. At Acre during the Third Crusade, Ambroise poetically described the conduct of their campaign:

> So delightful was the town,
> The wine so good, the girls so fair,
> All the soldiers lay down,
> And forgot the military affair.
> Wine and women cast their spell,
> Sunk in pleasure the men did dwell,
> In lechery and vice and sin.

In St Louis's Crusade, when Joinville asked the King why he had dismissed certain riotous soldiers, 'he replied that, to his own certain knowledge, and at a time when the army had never been in such distress, those whom he had dismissed had kept their brothels not a stone's throw from his own tent'. From King to the least menial who sharpened swords or held the horses, the influence of the new chivalry on the conduct of crusaders was hard to see.

The original purpose of chivalry was to govern and reform knighthood. But if it did not support the knight's traditional power, sustain his strength, and help him to command the battlefield, who would adhere to it? There is no doubt that the heavy cavalry of the western knights did not dominate the fights of the crusades with anything like their old, easy arrogance. There were those who con-

The Crusading knight, the typical Western heavy cavalryman with enveloping armour, large shield and long lance. From a 12th Cent fresco at Cressac, France.

tended that whatever success came out of the crusades resulted more from the determination and practicality of the 'little people' than from the strength of western knighthood. And certainly a knight who rushed about with precipitous gallantry did not show the military prudence so necessary against such a wily opponent as the Saracen. Chivalry was the virtue of knighthood: when the knight began to falter on the battlefield inevitably chivalry grew weak.

The individual knights lacked neither power nor bravery. The concerted charge of the Frankish heavy cavalry was still the most fearsome thing that the Saracens had ever seen, and they always tried to avoid that dreadful impact. On numerous occasions a tiny handful of knights was able to rout vastly superior forces. The downfall of the knights came through their devotion to feudal ways, their pride, their contempt for foot-soldiers, and their inability to adapt their tactics.

The crusaders conquered at first despite their military failings. Arab historians unanimously attributed this success to the anarchy of Islam, the Turkish emirs, the Fatamids of Egypt and the Abbasids of Baghdad being too busy feuding and plotting to combine against the common danger. 'While the Franks (God damn them!)' ibn al-Athir wrote bitterly, 'were conquering and settling in the lands of Islam, the rulers and armies of Islam were fighting among themselves.' Meanwhile, the Turks had already shown that the invaders were by no means invincible. The soldiers of Islam, among whom the Turks were by far the most formidable, relied on the speed, adaptability and cunning tactics of light horsemen. Their arms were not impressive; many a knight emerged from battle as bristly as a porcupine with Saracen arrows, but quite unharmed beneath his coat of mail.

But the Turks had perfected their tactics against the Byzantines and knew the vulnerable spots in the western formations. Impetuous heavy cavalry was lured to destruction by an enemy that would never stand and fight, but always fired and fled. Countryside was laid waste to deny food for the men and forage for the horses in the slow-moving western armies. Horses were deliberately shot from underneath the knights. Mounted knights were separated from the poorly protected foot-soldiers, then the Saracens would attack the infantry and destroy the westerners' base, their camp and equipment. But all the dangers posed by the Moslem troops might have been avoided by a little wisdom and a few precautions.

The feudal organization of both the crusading expeditions and the eastern kingdoms founded by the barons was a very great hindrance to military efficiency. The jealousies and divided loyalties within the large crusading armies prevented a unified plan and concerted action. The mercenary spirit of the vassals, with eyes ever-roving for plunder, effectively undid what little cooperation the leaders could achieve. The large armies never stayed long, and when they left the princes of the petty Christian kingdoms had to rely on the meagre feudal levies they could raise. William of Tyre said that the largest army the Latin kingdoms put into the field, to withstand Saladin in 1183, numbered fifteen thousand foot and a mere one thousand three hundred knights, and this was only done by denuding castles and towns of every last defender. At Jaffa in 1101, Baldwin I faced the whole Egyptian army with two hundred and forty knights and nine hundred infantry. At Ramla, in 1102, Baldwin had no infantry and gave battle with no more than three hundred knights. He was defeated. In 1118 the Franks undertook the invasion of Egypt with two hundred and sixteen knights and four hundred foot-men. They got to within three days of Cairo and returned safely to Palestine.

The chances of these pitiable battalions were never improved by the inveterate disdain of the knights for the infantry. A steady and balanced combination of infantry and cavalry was essential to defeat the tactics of the Saracen. But although the infantry formed by the ordinary pilgrims were available to crusading invasions in tens of thousands, and even the Christian kingdoms could raise a respectable number of foot-soldiers, no one learnt to use them sanely. They were useful for siege-warfare, for camp duties and for transport, but they were so despised that they were often left behind in battle. The class division between them and the knights was too absolute; warfare was the hereditary privilege of knighthood and the infantry was to have neither the booty nor the glory of battle.

'Sons of Islam,' cried the Iraqi poet al-Abiwardi, 'behind you are battles in which heads rolled at your feet. Dare you slumber in the blessed shade of safety, where life is as soft as orchard flowers? How can your eyes close amid disasters that would waken any sleeper?' With the coming of Zangi, Atabeg of Mosul and Aleppo, Islam awoke, and western power went into a long decline. And when Zangi retook the most northerly crusading state of Edessa in 1144, the event that brought on the Second Crusade, the omens of an ultimate Christian defeat were clear. Only the kingdom of Jerusalem and the two small states of Antioch and Tripoli remained, clinging to the coast and dependent on Italian sea-power for their very lives. The intervals of oriental intrigue that followed on the death of each Moslem strong man gave the crusaders temporary hope; but the next champion of Islam rose up remorselessly and checked western presumption. Neither the bravery of the leper-king Baldwin, the fierceness of Richard Lionheart, nor the dedication of St Louis could stop the slow strangulation of the Christian states. Saladin recaptured Jerusalem in September 1187, on 17 rajab which was the anniversary of Mohammed's ascension into heaven, and with the Holy City—the very symbol of crusading endeavour—lost, the efforts of the west became more desultory, more despairing, more hopeless.

In the early thirteenth century, the Mongol invasion and the dissensions of the Ayyubids gave the Christians a respite from which they tried to profit chiefly by attacks on Egypt, calculated to strike at the heart of Moslem power while the provinces were drowned in the blood of Mongol massacres. On two occasions Jerusalem reverted to the crusaders for a short time. But no wise man would build on such shallow success, caused by Moslem weakness. 'We are a war-like race,' the Sultan answered the challenge of St Louis in 1248; 'never is one of our champions cut down without being replaced. Fool! If your eyes had seen the points of our swords and the enormity of our devastations, the forts and shores we have taken, the lands we have sacked yesterday and today, you would gnaw your fingers in repentance!' With the accession of the Mamluk Sultan Baibars in twenty years, these words were powerfully confirmed. A general who could defeat the Mongols was no man to fear the Christians. Baibars and his successors Qalawun and al-Ashraf relentlessly destroyed the western possessions. Acre, the last stronghold, fell in June 1291, and the only surprise was that it had lasted that long. Europe, out of shame, frustration and failure, had for many years abandoned the principalities of the east. In an angry despair, the French poet Rutebeuf castigated the indifference of western knighthood: 'Jousters, what will you say on the Day of Judgment? How will you answer to God for His holy land? Oh Antioch, blessed territory, you cry out for a Godfrey. The fire of love is cold in the heart of each Christian.'

Long, long years of wasted effort, more defeats than victories, put Christian chivalry to flight. In general, the western knights (as also their Moslem enemy) fought with an ugly ferocity, cruel, treacherous, bloodthirsty. The most chivalrous warrior of the whole crusades was the Kurdish chief Saladin, whose orthodox piety, justice, resolution and magnanimity was a mirror in which western knighthood might perceive its lamentable deficiencies. The clemency of Saladin when he retook Jerusalem in 1187 contrasted very painfully with the overwhelming brutality of the Frankish conquest eighty-eight years before. 'His face shone with joy,' Imad ad-Din wrote truly of the leader he so much admired, 'his door was wide open, his benevolence spread far and wide.' Saladin had come to power in the ruthless manner of the east, but once enthroned he knew the humane duty of a prince.

Crusading warfare, so chivalrous in intention, brought out all the bad features of feudal fighting. 'Whoever has seen the Franks,' said Usama, 'has found them to be creatures superior in courage and ferocity, but in nothing else, just as animals are superior in strength and aggression.' The indiscipline and selfishness of feudal soldiers appeared all too clearly in the crusades. Early crusading armies had looted and pillaged their way to Constantinople and this bad precedent marked the conduct of the next two centuries. And the chances of booty in the rich cities of the Levant gave an extra temptation to riotous disorder which was not resisted. Ibn al-Qalanisi described a typical occasion at the capture of Tripoli in 1109: 'They sacked the city, captured the men, and enslaved the women and children. They seized vast quantities of loot and treasure as well as the contents of the city library, works of art and the heirlooms of the rich citizens.' Knights like Reynald of Châtillon, a not uncommon type, were no more than brigands, the crusading brothers of the robber-barons of Europe. From his great fortress at al-Karak, dominating the overland routes between Egypt and Syria, Reynald terrorized the countryside, plundering Christian Armenians and Moslems alike. He was cursed by Saracen and Christian, wrote William of Tyre, 'the Greeks as well as the Latins'. Handsome, treacherous, brave Reynald, whose looks and daredevil ways infatuated a princess, was the worst of a bad bunch. Others who shared his morals would have done as much evil had they also shared his sexual presence and his audacity.

Even more damnable than the rapacity of the knights was their cruelty and bloodlust. The slaughters of the crusades were the negation of chivalry, and the seal on its practical failure. The violent stain that dyed the first Crusaders at Antioch and Jerusalem disfigured their followers to the end. The Saracens fought a hard war, killing without compunction, but neither Zangi, nor Nur ad-Din, nor Saladin was particularly vengeful. Zangi stopped the riot of his army at Edessa in 1144; after Hittin, Saladin took vengeance against the Templars and Hospitallers only, and at Jerusalem he acted with the greatest restraint; prisoners were ransomed, women and children were enslaved according to the ordinary rules of eastern warfare, but there was no massacre. How different was the conduct of Richard Lionheart at the capture of Acre in 1191. The war-like qualities of the English King won the respect of all Moslems. He was, Baha ad-Din admitted, 'a man of great courage and spirit; one who had fought great battles and showed a burning passion for war'. He had received the surrender of the Moslem garrison at Acre; he had then promised to spare their lives, ransoming them or exchanging them for Christians held by Saladin. Having got both the ransom money and the Christian hostages, Richard decided to make a quick end of his prisoners. More than three thousand were led out in chains for the knights to fall on and murder in cold blood, with sword and lance.

The retaliation of blood for blood at last banished gallantry from both sides. The Egyptians murdered the sick and the prisoners from

Head of a young Crusader, from Montfort Castle, in Galilee.

St Louis's defeated army at Mansura and tossed the bodies to rot in the channels of the Nile. The crusading states died slowly amid brutalities too numerous to mention. The last opponents of the Christians were the Mamluks, a dynasty descended from slaves whom ibn Wasil called 'the Templars of Islam', which was a compliment to their courage and an acknowledgment of their ruthlessness. 'You would have seen', Baibars wrote to the Count of Tripoli, telling him that Antioch was lost, 'your Moslem enemy trampling on the place where you celebrate mass, cutting the throats of monks, priests and deacons upon the altars.' 'For this fate', said the Sultan, 'the River Orontes at first wept clear tears, but now the blood spilt into it has dyed them red'. The turn of Tripoli followed soon. In 1289 Qalawun blockaded it and battered it with catapults. After thirty-four days it fell, and the last defenders fled to the small island of St Thomas beyond the harbour. 'The Moslem troops', wrote Abu l-Fida who witnessed these events, 'flung themselves into the sea and swam with the horses to the island, where they killed all the men and took the women, children and goods. Afterwards I went by boat to the island, and found it heaped with putrefying corpses; we could not land for the stench.'

Acre, the last fortress, expired two years later after death-throes of mutual atrocity. A number of crusaders, chiefly Italians, had come to reinforce the city. Their first act of war was a massacre of the

Moslem farmers and peasants who brought supplies to the town market. 'These crusaders,' Gerard of Montreal wrote, 'who had come to help the city from charity and for the salvation of their souls, ended by causing its destruction.' In June 1291 al-Ashraf stormed Acre, putting to flight all the citizens except the Templars and Hospitallers who held out in fortified towers. After fierce resistance, seeing their case was hopeless, the Christians sued for their lives, a plea which the Sultan granted. But when they came out al-Ashraf ordered their execution, over two thousand of them, and to the last man they were beheaded outside the city walls. Acre fell, as the Moslem chroniclers quickly noted, on 17 jumada II, one hundred years to the day after Richard Lionheart had taken the city and given it the stain of its first massacre. The gory wheel came full circle—blood for blood, shame for shame brought the chivalrous enterprise of the crusades to a close.

# chapter six

The consecrated sword of knighthood, having failed in the Holy
Land, turned its edge on Europe. In the course of the twelfth
century the papacy had claimed the authority to lead Christendom,
and had very effectively demonstrated the right to this power by
zealous and successful promotion of the crusades. The Pope had his
reward, being at last acknowledged the leader of the west. The papacy
had won the great, wearisome struggle against the Holy Roman
Empire. The Church remained the only universal body in the western
world. Its authority was insistent and all-pervasive, and the Pope was
the master of this mighty house. But one thing marred his triumph.
At the moment when kings, barons and all the faithful gave way
before him, the obstinate mutterings of heresy in the lands of
Languedoc threatened the unity of his dominions. In a sombre work
of destruction, proving the theocratic power of the papacy, Pope
Innocent III turned against dissident Christians the weapon forged
for the harrying of Moslem infidels. And in doing so he used the
power of chivalry to destroy the land that gave birth to all that was

Pope Innocent III, the instigator of
the Albigensian Crusade, condemns
the heretic Amauri de Chartres.
From the 13th Cent *Grandes
Chroniques de France*.

fresh and joyful and sophisticated in the code of chivalry itself. He destroyed the culture and independent life of Languedoc.

Heresy came to the south in the same manner and by the same paths that the region had received its prosperity and its art. Heresy arrived stealthily from the east, by the trade routes, brought in by the mixture of peoples that jostled in the marts of the Mediterranean cities. When the south began to show the evidence of its bright life, signs of suspicious religious enthusiasm were also apparent. In 1119, the Council of Toulouse found itself in the midst of heretics. The Council of Rheims, in 1148, discovered that the infection had spread among 'the men who live in Gascony and Provence'. These were the souls in danger that St Bernard went to reclaim, and though his thundering denunciations drew listeners in thousands to the vast church of Albi, the heretics were not perturbed. After exhortation the Church tried punishment, condemning heretical initiates to life imprisonment, and threatening 'severer measures', while the ordinary followers were branded on forehead and cheek. Neither argument nor legal sanction had any effect. In 1163 the Council of Tours saw the south overrun with 'a damnable heresy' and directed all clergy of those parts to be 'on their guard' against heretics: 'let no one give them shelter under pain of anathema; let no one trade with them; let them be arrested and put in the custody of Catholic nobles, and their goods confiscated; let their meetings be strictly forbidden.' The more heresy was condemned, the better it flourished. 'The Arian heresy', wrote Roger of Hoveden in 1165, 'already condemned in the county of Toulouse, has just broken out again.'

Roger called these southern enthusiasts 'Arians', an orthodox term of abuse for a bundle of heresies, all with rather similar principles, originating in the east. These heretics, however, called themselves Cathars, the 'pure ones', and they became known to the rest of Europe as the Albigensians, named after Albi, the city at the point where the orthodox northern French stepped into the land of heresy. The Cathars chiefly differed from Catholics by a belief in the two opposing creative forces of Good and Evil. God was not omnipotent, but warred eternally with the Devil, who was surprisingly identified with Jehovah, the angry God of the Old Testament, demander of sacrifices and god of battles. Cathars also believed that Jesus was never incarnate, but only a kind of spiritual ghost, no more substantial than a projection on a screen, and consequently Mary was never his Mother, but also a phantom and perhaps only a symbol. Man, however, was only too clearly a creature of flesh and blood, a thing of gross appetites created by the Devil. All this was outrageous to Catholic doctrine. But as a final insult to orthodoxy the Cathars claimed that they, and not the Catholic Church, were the true successors to primitive Christianity, that the Church of Rome was the Whore of Babylon and all its sacraments, rites and ceremonies were not only worthless but abominable and blasphemous.

It is clear that the Cathars were not a timid group of doctrinal eccentrics, but rather a rival religion to Catholicism, bold and organized. They had their own 'priesthood' of the elect, the *perfecti*; they

The cathedral and town of Albi. The Albigensian Crusade took its name from this Southern town, and in this cathedral St Bernard tried and failed to turn back the current of Cathar heresy.

had their solemn rituals, in particular the *consolamentum*, the laying-on of hands that confirmed the elect; they had a notable band of preachers to spread the word; and they had a large following of ordinary men and women, the *credentes*, striving in austerity to reach the blessed brotherhood of *perfecti*. They were so strong they did not hesitate to summon their own church councils in the south, provocative counterblasts to the Catholic synods. In keeping with a gloomy view of human nature, the Cathar road to salvation was stony indeed. The *perfecti* were few, men and women in black robes signifying the mortification of the flesh and the withdrawal from the world. They had no churches, but set aside houses in each town where the *perfecti* lived, held their services, taught their doctrine, and cared for the poor and the sick.

The first mark of the *perfectus* was austerity. Utterly despising the things of the world, the elect were grave, composed, poor, given

Innocent III, papal autocrat, scourge of heretics, and patron of St Francis and St Dominic. From the painting by Giotto.

The corruption of the Church: an unworthy churchman is expelled from the church during the celebration of the Mass. From a 13th Cent manuscript.

to fasting and discipline worthy of an Indian fakir. The second mark was an upright goodness that won the elect the title of *les bons hommes*. Though the *perfecti* were dedicated to poverty, they had the use of funds provided by the followers, the *credentes*, and these they used exclusively for the benefit of their congregation. Cathars became especially adept at medicine; they would treat their own with loving devotion, but absolutely refuse to treat a Catholic. If the people were not convinced by the high moral standards of the Cathars, they were more easily persuaded by medical skills exclusively available within the Cathars. And the last mark of the *perfectus* was the conviction of his faith. St Bernard and St Dominic, two of the mightiest persuaders in the whole history of the Church, both preached to the Cathars in vain. In the appalling annals of the Inquisition, among the legion of Cathar names who died for their conviction, there are records of only three *perfecti* who renounced their faith, even though the stake and the fire awaited them all.

Cathar doctrine challenged the orthodoxy of the Church. But Cathar morality and goodness derided the decadence of the southern official hierachy, and this plain contrast made more recruits for heresy than any point of doctrine. When, in 1206, St Dominic began his mission among the Cathars he recognized that he must be as they were, poor, sober, unwearied, forever barefoot on the dusty roads of Languedoc, preaching, arguing, and persuading not only by good argument but also by good works. But this had never been the way of the southern clergy. Pope Innocent in Rome was aghast at their infamy: 'They are blind creatures,' he lamented, 'dumb hounds who can no longer bay, simoniacs who sell justice, damning the poor and giving absolution to the rich. They do not even keep the laws of the Church. They acquire endless benefices, entrusting the priesthood and Church offices to rogues and illiterate children. Hence the insolence of the heretics. Hence the contempt in which knights and villeins hold God and His Church.' With despair but without effect bishops and abbots were ordered to put on the habit and take off their robes and furs and jewels, to give up gaming and swearing and hunting and feasting, to stop excommunicating out of idle pique, to cease taking fees for ordinations and marriages, to get out of bed for Matins.

What the Pope saw from the distance of Rome was only too well known to the inhabitants of the south. 'The laity', wrote the southern chronicler Guillaume de Puylaurens, 'hold the priesthood in contempt, and the name of the priest, like that of Jew, has become part of a bad oath. The clergy are ashamed to show themselves and hide their tonsure by combing back their long hair. The nobles no longer put their sons into the priesthood, but advance the sons of menials.' The troubadour Peire Cardinal, who in the course of his very long life saw the full unfolding of the southern tragedy, raged against the sins of the clergy. 'Never did God have such enemies since time out of mind,' he wrote in one poem. He spoke of festering sins beneath smooth faces: 'They stop others doing what they enjoy, and instead of matins they have a new office, in which they lie with a whore until sunrise, and greet the day with bawdy song.' Caiaphas and Pilate, the poet concluded, 'will see God long before them'.

The shame of the clergy was too far gone to be redeemed in a short time even by a pope as powerful as Innocent III or a saint as dedicated as Dominic. 'The Church of Rome', a Cathar called Arnald Hot taunted St Dominic, 'was neither holy nor the Bride of Christ; it was the spouse of the Devil and its doctrine diabolical. It was that Babylon which St John in the Apocalypse called the mother of fornications and abominations, drunk with the blood of the saints and with Christ's martyrs.' The indictment, on the evidence of Languedoc, was extremely hard to refute; and compared to the Catholic clergy, the Cathar *perfecti* were very models of sanctity. So radiant were their virtues that the Count of Toulouse is said to have exclaimed, pointing to a crippled *perfectus* in rags: 'I would rather be this man than a king or emperor.' So convincing was their witness that the whole of Languedoc, from the Count of Toulouse himself to the meanest peasant, was permeated with Cathar doctrine. In 1145 St Bernard had found that the Catholic churches 'lack their congregations of the faithful; the faithful lack priests; the priests lack all honour'. Sixty years of preaching, culminating in the strenuous effort of St Dominic, could not win back the Catholics. There seemed but one thing to do for the unity of Christendom, and a certain biographer of Dominic recorded the frustrated Saint ominously threatening it: 'For some years now I have given you words of peace. I have preached, I have besought you with tears. But we have a proverb in Spain that where a blessing fails a stick will succeed. We will now rouse princes and prelates against you. And they, alas, will assemble whole nations and peoples, and a great number will

The sins of the clergy: the drunken monastic cellarer. From a 14th Cent manuscript.

Seal of Raymond VI, Count of Toulouse, the leader of the Southern forces against the Northern armies of the Albigensian Crusade.

die by the sword. Towers will fall, walls be razed, and all of you will be reduced to servitude. Thus force will prevail where gentle persuasion has failed.'

On 14th January 1208 Pierre de Castelnau, Papal Legate in the lands of heresy, was assassinated near Saint-Gilles by an officer of Raymond VI, Count of Toulouse. The provocation was too much for Pope Innocent. The spiritual weapons at his command had failed to subdue the heretics; his preachers were derided; excommunication was no threat to a land that hardly considered itself Catholic. For some years the Pope had tried to make Philip Augustus realize his theoretical responsibility as feudal overlord of the county of Toulouse, but the canny French King knew that his writ did not run in Languedoc. He was content to affirm his rights as suzerain and await the outcome of whatever action the Pope might take. If the temporal arm would not work for him, the Pope would have to enforce his own authority. He had, as a last resort, the power to summon a crusade, and with his usual resolution Innocent hardly hesitated to do so. On 10th March 1208 he declared a holy war against a people who were fellow Christians, but Christians anathematized by the Pope as 'worse than the very Saracens'.

The direction of the crusade was entrusted to Arnaud-Amalric, Abbot of Cîteaux, a violent, ambitious southerner who preached the destruction of the Cathars with fierce enthusiasm. Bearing the blood-stained white habit of the murdered Legate, Arnaud-Amalric

The seal of Simon de Montfort, military leader of the Albigensian Crusade.

roused the knighthood of France, a land (as the chronicler said) 'that has ever fought in God's cause', offering indulgences 'equal to those usually granted to crusaders who crossed the seas to bring help to the Holy Land'. And those who could not be persuaded by promises, Arnaud-Amalric intimidated with curses. The *Chanson de la Croisade* recorded the following malediction: 'May the man who abstains from this crusade never drink wine again; may he never eat, morning or evening, off a good cloth, or dress again in fine stuff until the end of his days; and at his death may he be buried like a dog!' A large army of crusaders, chiefly Frenchmen, but Normans, Flemish, Burgundians also, and not a few knights from Languedoc as well, gathered at Lyons.

The smooth tones of the historian, which studiously avoid passion, nevertheless become agitated by the events of the Albigensian Crusade, regret and distaste mixed in equal parts. The attack of kinsman on kinsman, the infamy of Christian against Christian! The conscience of the thirteenth century was not particularly troubled: why should it be? To men of deep conviction, heresy was the ultimate abomination. To many, the heretic was worse than the Saracen, for the infidel had never known the faith but the heretic had spurned it. Simon de Montfort, the stern general against the Albigensians, had abandoned the Fourth Crusade at Zara in 1203, because his conscience would not allow him to plunder Christians under cover of a crusade. But he undertook the campaign against the Cathar heretics with a religious devotion that made him all the more terrible as an opponent. For the knight who believed in military chivalry, the Albigensian Crusade was both timely and attractive. The crusades in the Holy Land were plagued with failure and attended by shame; the recent, treacherous conquest of Constantinople by the Fourth Crusade was an ugly blot on the reputation of western knighthood. In Languedoc, the principles of military chivalry in support of true faith might be conveniently re-asserted. Here was a cancer actually within the body of Christ's Church. Here was a goal so close and familiar, it seemed a knight might reach it and do his work without being perplexed or turned aside by the intricate problems of the east.

So reasoned the men of good faith. For the rest, no doubt the bulk of the crusaders, the campaign seemed just another joyous occasion for feudal war, for adventure, plunder and conquest. Unhappily for simple desires, complex calculations upset all the crusaders, both the knights of conscience and the feudal brawlers. Most of the land of Languedoc was a feudal anomaly, owing theoretical allegiance to two or more of the three kingdoms of France, England and Aragon. Yet the barons of the region were notoriously independent, strident defenders of their own rights, jealous of neighbours, contemptuous of their remote overlords. In a land of Christian scandal, such great lords as Raymond, Count of Toulouse, and Raymond-Roger Trencavel, Viscount of Béziers, were not likely to be religious. Indeed, Count Raymond was known to have had five wives, two of whom were living. Natural sinners, they were still unconvicted of heresy, but it was also no secret that they encouraged the Cathars, for the heretics were good people and the heresy was the distinctive faith of the south, a symbol of southern independence. So the crushing of heresy became also an opportunity for a strong overlord to put down wilful vassals; and when Philip Augustus, the most resourceful monarch of Europe, saw the chance to consolidate his kingdom he took it. Behind the skirts of orthodoxy, the young French giant triumphed over the artful but fragmented feudatories of the south. And this state-conquest was made easier, and more terrible, by the nature of the holy war. Feudal wars were in general affairs of short duration and limited terror; once honour and greed were satisfied, the victor departed and the defeated breathed again. But religious war expressed a cruel new logic: the heretic must recant or die; the obdurate must be pursued to the end of time, caught, and exterminated, and any who helped or befriended them were liable to die also. 'Kill them all,' Arnaud-Amalric is said to have cried at the first battle of the Crusade; 'God will look after His own.' The fratricidal war of religion condemned the chivalrous knight to become a ritual executioner.

In July 1209, after a year of plot and preparation, the great army of crusaders advanced south. To the author of the *Chanson de la*

The Albigensian Crusaders capture Béziers on 22 July 1209. Here, for the first time, the South felt the brutal force of the Northern Crusading knights and their mercenary troops. From the *Chanson de la Croisade.*

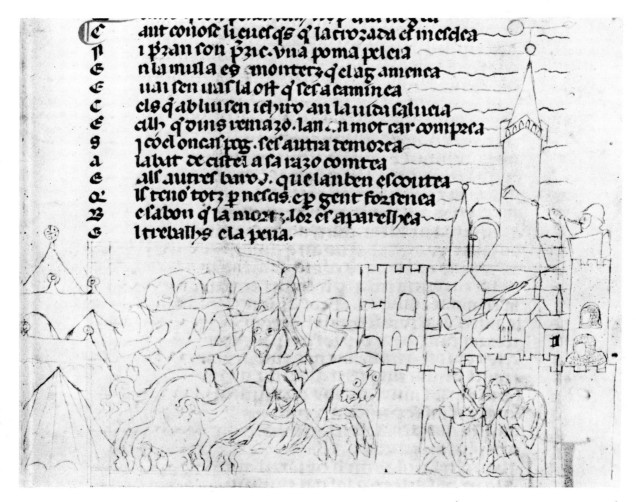

*Croisade*, the transports of the invaders seemed to make the Rhône solid, and the multitude of the marching host—knights, clergy, pilgrims, mercenaries—made a sea of the land. Count Raymond, having failed to prevent the invasion and having suffered humiliation, public penance and scourging by the hand of the Church, thought it prudent to join, and appeared at Valence in the crusader's cross. The nominal enemy now seemed to be Raymond-Roger Trencavel, and this baron, demoralized by the duplicity of his old compatriot of Toulouse, retreated to Béziers, exhorted the town to resist and then dashed to his chief city Carcassone. The Catholic citizens of Béziers determined to resist, for they did not understand the true significance of the crusade. They thought they were engaged in normal feudal warfare such as they had seen many times. They saw chiefly an attempt by the northern French to attack their liberties, and they were prepared to join with the heretical Cathars to withstand these presumptuous northerners. On 22nd July, the Feast of Mary Magdalene, Béziers was taken, mainly owing to the foolishness of the defenders, and the citizens of the south learnt for the first time the bitter reality of crusading warfare. The usual instinct of mercenaries abetted the stern sword of orthodoxy. Catholic and Cathar alike fled to the haven of the church, but they were pulled out indiscriminately and slaughtered. The French mercenaries, the hardened and savage *routiers*, 'were fierce for plunder, and had no fear of death; they cut the throats of any who stood in their way'.

The south became a land convulsed by nightmare. Carcassone was spared to become the crusaders' stronghold, but Raymond-Roger Trencavel was captured and soon died, of dysentery or poisoned. His fiefs of Béziers and Carcassone were given to the Anglo-Norman knight Simon de Montfort, who then assumed the military responsibility for the completion of the crusade. De Montfort was a general in the powerful line of Norman soldiers. His ancestry and training had made him the hardest of warriors, and his crusader's faith made him merciless to heretics. For the length of the campaign, after the large army of pilgrims had melted back to their homes, de Montfort had to rely on a few chivalrous knights, fighting for religion, and a larger number of *routiers* of proved bestiality, fighting for plunder. The first act of the war, the massacre at Béziers, had paralysed the enemy, and by deliberate policy, knowing the limited forces they would have in the future, the crusaders decided to run a campaign of terror. 'The nobles of France,' William of Tudela expressly recorded, 'clergy and laity, princes and marquises, were agreed amongst themselves that whenever a castle refused to surrender, and had to be taken by force, the inhabitants were all to be put to the sword and slain, thinking that afterwards no man would dare to oppose them by reason of the fear that would go abroad when it was seen what they had already done.'

The first inrush of the crusaders won brilliant military success. But the real work, the rooting out of heresy, had hardly begun. The Cathar *perfecti* took off their tell-tale black robes and appeared as ordinary citizens; their sympathizers either feigned Catholicism or retired to remote mountain forts. For ten years Simon de Montfort

Carcassone: this city, though deep in the lands of the Cathars, was spared the destruction suffered by so many great Southern towns and cities, because the Crusading general Simon de Montfort made Carcassone his headquarters.

waged a campaign of persevering brutality against a vanishing enemy. There were scenes of extraordinary horror on both sides. The Cathars, knowing what to expect from the crusaders, retaliated in kind. The chronicler Pierre des Vaux-de-Cernay spoke of Catholic altars defiled, of a priest chopped in pieces. The *Chanson de la Croisade* has the Albigensian champion, the Count of Foix, boasting of his murders: 'All those that I slew or destroyed filled my heart with gladness.' At Lavaur, unarmed German crusaders were surprised and massacred; at Montgey, more than a thousand people, said to be Catholic pilgrims, were slain. Simon de Montfort, to the enthusiastic partisan Vaux-de-Cernay, was a prince of chivalry, but to an anonymous chronicler of the south he was a blood-stained tyrant. Certainly, under the tireless command of this huge Norman dreadful atrocities were committed. At Minerve, one hundred and forty *perfecti* flung upon a great fire. At Lavaur, four hundred *perfecti*, men and women, burnt, the defender Aimery de Montréal and eighty of his knights hanged, and the chatelaine of the fortress, the gallant *perfecta* Guiraude de Laurac, cast in a well with rocks hurled upon her.

In September 1213, de Montfort won a decisive victory at Muret over Pedro of Aragon and the Count of Toulouse (who had soon deserted the crusaders who were raping his land). In 1215, the Fourth Lateran Council vigorously approved the bloodthirsty conduct of the crusade, confirmed de Montfort in his new power and

The citizens of Toulouse welcome their count to the city: the Southern chronicler leaves no doubt as to the popularity of Raymond VI in his own land. From the 13th Cent *Chanson de la Croisade*.

titles, and sent the general back to complete the eradication of heresy. In June 1218, the most hated foreigner Simon de Montfort was killed at the siege of Toulouse, killed, said the *Chanson de la Croisade*, by a missile from the women who defended the walls: 'A stone flew straight to its proper mark, and smote Count Simon on his steel helm, so that his eyeballs, brains, teeth, skull and jawbone all flew into pieces, and he fell down upon the ground stark dead, blackened and bloody.' That was the joyful revenge of the south, and for a while it seemed as if the crusade would fail. But the King of France had invested de Montfort in the dispossessed lands of Toulouse, tacitly supporting the aims of the crusade, and making known his interest in an ultimate victory over the southern barons. Philip Augustus died in 1223. The new King, Louis VIII, having claimed the lands of Toulouse and being confirmed in them by Pope Honorius III, took the cross in 1226 and brought the full weight of the French kingdom, backed by the full authority of the Church, against the decimated but still defiant south. Though there were many painful years still to go, the issue could not be in doubt. In 1233, the followers of St Dominic brought the Inquisition to Languedoc, and oppressed with fire where their master had failed with the word. On 16th March 1244 the garrison of the last Cathar fortress at Montségur capitulated, and the elect were dragged chanting down the mountain slope to the place still called today the *Champs de*

Pope Gregory instructs the Dominicans to establish the Inquisition in the lands of the Cathars, 1232. From the *Decretals* of Gregory IX, *c.* 1280.

The Castle of Montségur, the Cathar stronghold in the rugged foothills of the Pyrenees, and the last outpost of Cathar resistance during the Albigensian Crusade.

*Cramatchs*, the 'field of the burnt'. Here an immense pyre awaited them, logs and faggots mixed with straw and pitch, to help combustion in the damp March of the Pyrenees. When the pyre was well lit, two hundred heretics were tossed into it. Through the hours of darkness the vast conflagration made the night sky lurid, while the little mocking camp-fires of the crusaders winked round the great sacrifice.

It was a comprehensive devastation. By one account, a million dead in thirty-five years of intermittent war. Toulouse, the greatest city of the south, a place in ruins, sighing with mourning women and useless elders. Béziers utterly burnt, 'so fierce were the flames, the cathedral that Master Gervais built burst asunder, cracked down the middle, and fell in two'. Lesser towns pillaged and empty. Limoux, Castres, Pamiers become fiefs to northern barons and despoiled by extortionate taxes. The great castles of the courtly life—Termes, Fanjeaux, Lavaur, Minerve—broken and razed, or harshly occupied by exulting Frenchmen. The countryside systematically stripped of crops and vines so that famine and destitution were the peasant's lot. The valleys of the Ariège for six years annually ravaged by de Montfort. The people successfully deprived of livelihood, the land deprived of the trade that had made it prosperous.

The affair that began for the correction of heresy became the rape and the punishment of the south. Behind the spiritual foe, the Cathar heretics, lay more palpable political enemies, Raymond VI and Raymond VII of Toulouse, men not even convicted of heresy but damned for independence; and obscurely behind the counts of Toulouse lay the fundamental enemy, the anarchic southern life, the individual conduct of a land with divergent social, political and religious thought, a conduct that threatened the mighty orthodoxies of papal religion and French statehood.

Made wise by suffering, the chroniclers of the south perceived something of the true state of the war, and refused to give the campaign the dignity of religious warfare. They knew how easy it was for an ambitious knight to sniff heresy in a town or fief he coveted. They saw Catholic and Cathar fighting side by side, without distinc-

One result of the Cathar troubles was the gradual loss of manorial lands by the Southern nobility. Here are the seals from two transfers of land to the powerful Order of the Templars: *left*, Guillaume de Forcalquier donates land at Manosque, 1206; *right*, Raembaut d'Orange donates land at le Comtat, 1215.

tion of faith, against a northern invasion. 'We were all raised together,' said the Catholic Pons Adhémar; 'many of them are related to us. And we can see for ourselves that they lead decent, honourable lives.' They saw how fiercely Catholic women, even girls, defended the walls of Toulouse, knowing very well what to expect from the *routiers* of de Montfort's army. They identified the enemy quite clearly as *Francès et clergia*, power-hungry Frenchmen and decadent priests, 'these thieves,' said the Count of Foix, 'these traitors without faith or honour who wear the cross that has been our ruin'. To the chroniclers, the contest was between foreign power, the overweening, sullen, puritan power of papacy and resurgent France, and those indefinable southern attributes that were called in the Languedoc *pretz* and *paratge*, loosely translated as 'joy, honour, chivalry'. In 1216, when the Count of Toulouse and his son renewed the fight against de Montfort, they promised their supporters 'the esteem of all Christendom, for you are bringing back chivalry and joy and *paratge*'.

Unhappily for the south, the strong Church of Innocent III no longer saw chivalry as the glory of Christendom. Chivalry belonged to the feudal past, an eccentric, pleasure-loving, antiquated relic. It was a licence that must be put away in the interest of discipline, orthodoxy and unified power, the new virtues of papacy and monarchy alike. In this matter, Folquet of Marseilles demonstrated the drift of history. Folquet began life as a troubadour, one of the greatest writers of Provençal love lyrics. In 1195 he entered a Cistercian monastery, repudiating his past so thoroughly that he did penance when he heard his old songs performed. By the time of the Albigensian Crusade he was no longer the poet Folquet, but the Frenchified Foulques, Bishop of Toulouse, champion of orthodoxy and upholder of de Montfort so that the chroniclers of his own south execrated him for spreading 'such fire in the land that no amount of water will ever quench it'. The past was *paratge* and chivalry, the subtle apprehension of gusty and capricious emotions, love and service of women, fruits of the pen, sounds of the rebec, baying of dogs, mewing of the hawk on the fist, the incomprehensible moods of

Departure for the Crusade. To avoid the difficult land route, Crusaders had, by the 13th Cent, taken to transport by ships, often provided by the Italian city-states, a method that was quick and relatively safe, but expensive for the feudal lord. From the *Statutes of the Order of the Holy Spirit of Naples.*

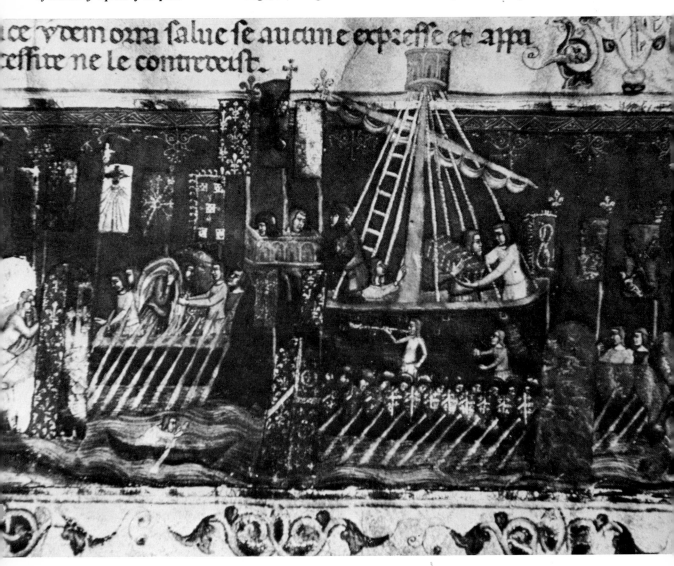

sunlight between dawning and dying. The future was subjection of the spirit, humble submission to the authority of the Church, severity in the cause of orthodoxy, the hard friendship of St Dominic and the steady support of the mortifying Dominican Inquisition, and at last, after all pains and all fury, the famous approbation of Dante, for whom Folquet was in Paradise, the servant of the new way, 'the shining and precious jewel of our heaven'.

The world went by leaving the once-mighty knight puzzled, less powerful, more impoverished. The expense of chivalrous enterprise was very great, yet income from domain lands was constantly falling in value. To bear his part in the First Crusade, Godfrey of Bouillon had to sell the fiefs of Mouzon and Stenay, and mortgage the duchy of Bouillon itself to the monks of Liège. And most crusaders, from prince to poor knight, according to his means, had to make a similar financial sacrifice. But later crusaders were to find the cost beyond their diminishing revenues. War-horse, weapons and armour had always been dear. Robert de Clary, a chronicler of the Fourth Crusade, found his humble six hectares of land in Picardy insufficient to support knightly accoutrements, and had the indignity of crusading as a mere foot-soldier. But equipment was only the beginning of expense. There was also transport, victualling and maintenance to consider. A poor knight generally attached himself to the *mesnie*, the household band, of his lord, and relied on him for support. Thus the burden of feudal leadership could be very heavy. In 1248, to take himself, his men and all his equipment to the Holy Land, Count Jean de Dreux hired the Marseilles ship *La Bénite* for two thousand pounds *tournois*. Another ship, *La Bonne Aventure*, cost Guy de Forez nine hundred and seventy-five silver marks.

The campaign itself consumed treasure prodigally. Philip Augustus put the bare maintenance of one soldier for one year at a hundred and sixty-five silver marks. Joinville, Seneschal of Champagne and a baron of adequate wealth, found his crusading responsibilities too much for his purse. One thousand pounds a year was not enough for himself and his nine knights. At Cyprus, before ever setting foot in the Holy Land, he was rescued by the generosity of St Louis, and later he could not go on without further support from the King: he needed four hundred pounds each for three new knights, and another eight hundred pounds 'to mount and arm myself and feed my knights, for you would not have us feed at your lodgings'. Joinville's effort in the Holy Land had brought him and his people to the edge of ruin, and when St Louis approached him to join another crusade to Tunis, he protested his devotion to religion and his willingness to serve the King, but frankly admitted that he could not afford it, for he and his people were so impoverished 'that the day would never come when they and I would not suffer the effect'. The bankruptcy of Joinville was typical enough; it was his chivalrous conduct and steadfast loyalty to the crusading ideal that had become rare.

Desperate for money, the knight looked to plunder to make up his losses, or fell into the hands of the rising class of merchants. From the twelfth century onwards the crusades could not have continued

Western soldiers of the Fourth Crusade. Arms and armour are largely unchanged from two centuries before: enveloping chain-mail surcoat, kite-shaped shield, and long spear or lance. From a mosaic in Ravenna, dated *c.* 1213.

without the support of trading cities, and the campaigns of knight-errancy in reality had as much to do with commercial expansion as with holy warfare. The Italian city-states, where capitalism was born, saw immediately the advantage of Christian ports in the rich Levant, and for a price lent their navies and resources to the naïve crusaders. Sidon and Tyre would not have fallen without the Venetians. Laodicea and Tripoli were taken with the help of the Pisans. Genoa plotted the downfall of Caesarea, Tortosa, Acre and Beirut.

At length merchant complicity interfered further in the affairs of chivalry, and the influence of Venice determined the ignoble course of the Fourth Crusade. The city had contracted to supply transport and provisions for the whole crusading army, at a cost of ninety-four thousand silver marks. When the crusaders, improvident as usual, found themselves thirty-four thousand marks short, Venice offered to waive the remainder if only the crusade would re-capture the Adriatic island-town of Zara from the King of Hungary. The crusaders reluctantly agreed, and did this piece of dirty work despite the anathema of the Pope, and, once fallen, found it impossible to resist when Venice insinuated into their path the far greater temptation of the Byzantine Empire. Recklessly embroiled with a rival claimant to the Byzantine throne, the crusade swept on to

The conquest of Constantinople by the Latin knights of the Fourth Crusade. The artist implies the treachery and brutality of the Crusading knights against the innocent Greeks of the city. From a mosaic in Ravenna, dated c. 1213.

Constantinople and crowned a puppet king, only to see him soon displaced by another usurper. By this time the voracious crusaders were under the spell of a city infinitely grander than any in the west. 'They were not able to believe', wrote Villehardouin, 'that there could be so rich a town in the whole world, those high walls and mighty towers, those luxurious palaces and lofty churches.' Venetians and crusaders decided to annex these riches, to share the booty of conquest, leaving a Latin kingdom under crusader rule while Venice would get what she most desired, the fabulous trade of the

Sack of a town: the enmity between townsmen and the rural petty nobility gradually increased throughout the Middle Ages. From the *Chroniques de Froissart*, late 14th Cent.

golden city. On 12th April 1204 Constantinople was taken and the looting began, appropriately led (wrote the poor foot-soldier Robert de Clary) by the greatest barons: 'Every rich man took either jewels or gold or silken stuff, and nothing was ever given to the ordinary soldiers, nor to the poor knights, nor to the sergeants who had helped

win the city.' The whole enterprise was tainted with the infection of greed, and those who had spent most spurned all chivalry and angrily fought for the best of the plunder.

That merchants should determine a crusade was a sign of the new importance of trade and the new power of the cities. The feudal knight was a country gentleman, bound to land, having a limited income from land, and rigidly placed in the social hierarchy of landholding. In the cities of northern Italy and southern France, in the Flemish towns of the Low Countries, there grew up with great rapidity a new social organization based on town life and on trade. The leaders of this new organization were the merchants, men motivated solely by the hope of gain, freemen employing free labour, dealing in money rather than service or kind, men quite outside the agricultural bondage of the countryside, free from both the ideals and the restrictions of feudalism. The bourgeois—the town-dweller—was a complete stranger to both noble and peasant, and the men of the land, both rich and poor, distrusted and feared this interloper who so casually contradicted the whole philosophy of their being. The strength and exclusiveness of the town commune was a terrible thing to the rural knight. 'Not only do they crush and ruin the knights and the countryside,' Jacques de Vitry wrote of the communes, 'taking away the lord's jurisdiction over his men, but they even usurp the rights of the Church and demolish the independence of the clergy by their iniquitous statutes, contrary to all canonical law.'

But the future was with the townsmen. Trade brought a sudden increase in population which swelled the towns but left the country untouched. Kings, who had at first resisted the rise of the cities, at last saw them as a source of power to strengthen the central government of monarchy and weaken the independent presumption of great feudal vassals. The royal coffers caught some of the bountiful overflow from trading profits, and the royal administration benefited from the quicker wits and better education of the townsmen. As the town went up, the country went down. The closed system of feudal dependence, from villein to lord, was burst apart by the start of a money economy. Why should a peasant give service in bondage when he might be a free man working for a money wage? The money that poured from the multitudes in the towns disordered the peasants with hopes of profit and freedom. And that same money, by continually raising the cost of living, crippled the petty military nobility who depended on fixed revenues from their lands.

By the thirteenth century, western knighthood, unwisely spendthrift in the campaigns of the crusades and severely squeezed by the new economy, was little more than a congregation of paupers. Knighthood itself was for sale, just another commodity of the marketplace; 'soapsellers and their sons', said *Piers Plowman*, 'for silver have been knights.' The honour was so devalued, many tried to disown it. When Edward I enacted, in 1278, that all English freeholders of more than twenty pounds a year must take up knighthood, the provision was widely evaded. The small knight, a ragged noble dwelling on past glories, was often reduced to a beggar at the rich townsman's door. 'The city usurer', wrote the poet John Gower, 'maintains his brokers and procurers, who search out knights, vavasours and squires. When these have mortgaged their lands and are driven by need to debt, then these rascals lead them to the usurer.'

With honour and income declining, the knight easily fell from the high expectations of chivalry. His office, as Ramon Lull reminded him at the end of the thirteenth century, was to redress wrongs and affirm the truth: 'It behoveth him that by love he recover charity and instruction, and by fear recover virtue and justice.' His devotion was given to his faith, to his lord, and to the people; and the safety of the people was not the least of these cares, seeing how poor and vulnerable they were. 'The office of a knight,' Lull wrote, 'is to maintain and defend women, widows and orphans, and sick men and those not puissant nor strong. For like as custom and reason is that the greatest and most mighty help the feeble and less, and that they have recourse to the great. Right so is the order of chivalry, by cause she is great, honourable and mighty, be in surrour and in aid to them that be under him and less mighty and less honoured than he is.' Out of the responsibility of his place, the knight saved, protected and preserved his people, while they in return gave him their service. The homely peasant in *Piers Plowman* instructed the knight thus:

I shall work and sweat and sow for us both,
And other labours do for they love, all my lifetime,
In covenant that thou keep Holy Church and myself
From wasters and wicked, that this world destroy.

'If I wished to do God's will,' Joinville told those who urged him to crusade once more, 'I should stay at home to help and protect my people; for were I to endanger my person in the pilgrimage of the Cross, knowing full well that it would be against the well-being of my people, I should incur the anger of God, who gave His life to save His people.' Such a statement of affectionate care was rare indeed in the thirteenth century. Even Lull, the enthusiast of chivalry, admitted the falling away from the knightly ideal. The knights of his age, he wrote, 'disordain the order of chivalry': 'All the knights now injurious and proud, full of wickedness, be not worthy to chivalry, but ought to be reputed for nought.' And Sir Gilbert Hay, a sharp-tongued translator of Lull, scornfully suggested that more would be drawn to chivalry if it commanded the oppression of the poor, for so many were irked by the need to practise 'loyalty, courtesy, liberality, love and pity'.

The evidence of history gave the theorists sufficient grounds for their laments. 'Who has not seen', Giraut de Borneil wrote around 1200, 'racks of torture, or villeins forced into knightly service? Now only those who pillage or rob sheep are prized. Shame on the knight who protests his courtly love fresh from a raid on bleating lambs, or with stolen money from churches or pilgrims in his pocket.' Peire Cardinal, who had seen southern chivalry crushed on the field of Muret in 1213, saw a world in ruins: 'Great barons pity others as Cain did Abel; they steal more readily than wolves and lie more easily than whores. From orient to setting sun, with anyone I'll strike a bargain: to a loyal man I'll give a besant if all the disloyal give me a nail; to courtly men I'll give a mark of gold if the ill-mannered give me a pound *tournois*; to the truthful I'll give heaps of riches if I can have an egg for every liar. All the laws such men observe I could write on a scrap of parchment, on half the thumb of my glove.' Guiraut Riquier, called the last of the troubadours, writing at the end of the century, feared a world overrun by the devil and the Saracens, so badly had western knighthood failed in its duty to faith and polity.

Feudalism hardly working, the knight degenerate—from the start of the thirteenth century there were bad times for the peasants. They were the easiest victims, made to atone for the poverty and enfeeblement of their masters. Those who should have protected them found it simpler to prey on them. Many knights, wrote that indignant social observer Jacques de Vitry, forced their villeins to labour without bread, and, still more tyrannical, seized whatever poor goods the peasants collected: 'Many say nowadays, when they are rebuked for taking the peasant's cow, "Let it suffice the churl that I've left him his calf and his life. I could do him more harm if I cared. I've taken this goose but left him the feathers." ' To be robbed by the very man who held you in bondage was the most bitter oppression of all, and it is no wonder that the peasants began to cry out against the tied servitude of the feudal system. 'We are men formed in Christ's likeness,' says one pathetic villein in Froissart, 'and we are kept like beasts.' Once more, the candid witness of *Piers Plowman* gives the indictment of the meek against the terror of the petty rural nobility:

And how he ravaged Rose, Reginald's leman,
And Margaret of her maidenhead, maugre her cheeks.
'Both my geese and my griskins his gadlings fetchen,
I dare not for dread of him fight nor chide.
He borrowed my bay steed, and brought him never again,
Nor no farthing him for, for nought I can plead.
He maintaineth his men to murder mine own,
Forestalleth my fair, fighteth in my markets,
Breaketh up my barn-door and beareth away my wheat;
And taketh me but a tally for ten quarter oaten;
And yet he beat me thereto, and lieth by my maiden,
I am not so hardy for him up for to look.'

All this was but the sombre fulfilment of a knightly tyranny that Peter of Blois had detected beginning long before, rooted in the pride and violence of knighthood. 'Knights of old', he wrote around 1170, 'bound themselves by oath to support the state, not to flee from battle, and to put the public good before their own lives. But all goes by contraries, for nowadays, from the moment when they are honoured with the knightly belt, they rise up against the Lord's anointed and rage against the patrimony of the Crucified. They rob and despoil Christ's poor, afflicting the wretched miserably and without mercy, that from other men's pains they may gratify their unlawful appetites and wanton pleasures. They who should have used their strength against Christ's enemies fight now in their cups and drunkeness, waste time in sloth, moulder in debauchery, and dishonour the name and office of knighthood by their degenerate lives.'

Having failed in the crusades, failed in the defence of true faith, failed in social duty to the commonwealth, the knights at last suffered the most calamitous fall of all, being found wanting in their proper business, which was the command of the European battle-field. When they lost their military power they lost all chivalry.

The code of chivalry thought of warfare as an elegant contest for opposing forces of heavy cavalry, played out by aristocratic partici-pants. The game was dangerous enough to give a spice to bold lives, but not sufficiently dangerous to make the odds unattractive. An armoured knight was hard to kill, and an opponent greatly preferred the profit of a ransom to the dubious satisfaction of a killing. The chivalrous battles between mounted knights were small affairs of limited damage. At Tinchebrai, in 1106, Henry I of England won Normandy without losing a single knight. At Bouvines in 1214, when Philip Augustus broke the continental power of England in one of the crucial battles of the Middle Ages, the vanquished lost a mere hundred and seventy knights. In these grave contests between states

A scene of brigandage from the Hundred Years War: the fighting of this long campaign grew increasingly bestial, chiefly owing to the savage indiscipline of mercenary companies. From a 15th Cent manuscript, by Gauthier de Coincy.

the eye of the knight was on ransom money, and in lesser skirmishes the eye was chiefly on plunder.

In time an alien and savage element crept into these gallant demonstrations, an element that brought greater treachery and rapacity and more certain death. It was a hard expense in time and money for a chivalrous knight to undertake a long campaign or one far from home, and so it slowly became the custom to hire mercenaries when knights were difficult to find. The terror that the mercenary, or *routier*, inspired was one of the marks of the Albigensian Crusade. For he did not share the chivalry of the knight; he was a ragged professional, usually a foot-soldier, a barefoot murderer and pillager, seemingly indifferent to pain and to death, quite without morals or discipline, so treacherous and dangerous that the Church tried to ban his use. But he was conveniently at hand and anxious to work, and as knights became less and less able to bear the burdens of their rank the *routiers* found more and more employment until finally they formed the truly bestial 'free companies' of the Hundred Years War, winning such nicknames as 'The Flayers' and the like.

Inevitably, the *routiers* dragged down the chivalry of the knights and infected warfare with their own disgusting standards. Christine de Pisan, in her fourteenth-century *Deeds of Arms and Chivalry*, found a great increase in the pillaging, not only of enemy lands, but of friendly territory also, which she severely condemned: 'Such folk ought better to be called thieves and robbers than men of arms or chivalrous.' And the frequency of slaughter brought a new callousness towards death. Froissart relates the infamous occasion at Aljubarrota, in 1385, when the Portuguese and English allies murdered their French and Spanish prisoners; 'Behold the great evil adventure that befell that Saturday,' the chivalrous historian wrote, recalling other days and other manners; 'for they slew as many prisoners as would well have been worth, one with another, four hundred thousand franks!' At Agincourt, Henry V, fearful of the great body of prisoners he had collected, also arranged a hasty execution.

While *routiers* degraded war, England prepared further military blows to chivalry. The restricted class of knighthood was no longer able to supply sufficient soldiers. France, the pre-eminent land of chivalry, still relied on ranks of knights complemented by the savage but unreliable companies of *routiers*. But England, smaller and poorer, staking her power not on the hereditary privilege of an aristocracy, but on the national fervour of the whole country, under Edward I reintroduced the old principle of general conscription, making every sound, male citizen a partaker in military enterprise. The Statute of Winchester and various Assizes of Arms, rigorously applied, cautioned every man to possess certain weapons and to be trained in their use. At the end of the thirteenth century this citizen-army was hardened in the wars against the Scots. When Edward III began the first part of the Hundred Years War in France, he had a large, vigorous body of well-trained men, united under a strong king and anxious for the reputation of their country. For the first time since chivalry began, a nation rather than a class was at war, and the ambition of a land greedy for riches and glory was an ominous threat to feudal chivalry.

And to support the aggressive national will, England at last had a new weapon and new tactics. The advent of the long-bow, together with the tactical disposition of cavalry balanced by dismounted men-at-arms and arrow-firing foot-soldiers, brought to an end nearly a thousand years during which heavy cavalry had dominated the western battlefield.

The long-bow is said to have come from Wales, being one of the prizes that Edward I brought back from his Welsh campaign in the late thirteenth century. The power of this bow had long been known to the men of the border-lands; in 1182 the Welsh chronicler Giraldus Cambrensis spoke of arrows penetrating a four-inch oak door, and of a knight pierced through mail-shirt, mail-breeches, thigh, wooden saddle and horse's flank by one arrow. But English armies had always used the slow, unwieldly continental cross-bow, handled by mercenaries, and it was not until Edward and his cavalry were under the painful flights of Welsh arrows that they learnt the advantage of the long-bow and the difficulty of heavily encumbered knights in avoiding rapid flights of arrows poured on them from a long range. Edward, a man of real military talent, quickly learnt his lesson, and ordained these 'ugly, unfinished-looking weapons, astonishingly stiff, large and strong' (as Giraldus called them) for the use of his new citizen-militia. At Bannockburn, in 1314, the English tried for the last time to crush the enemy by a reckless rampage of heavy cavalry, and suffered from the steady Scottish infantry a most

*Right*. The Battle of Crécy. On the right are the English longbowmen whose power, accuracy and rapidity of fire largely determined the day. On the left are the cumbersome and slow crossbows of the Genoese mercenaries who failed to make any impression on the English. From the late 14th Cent *Chroniques de Froissart*.

*Below*. The Battle of Agincourt, from the *Vigils de Charles VII*.

grans seigneurs que chun vouloit
monstrer sa puissance. Si nest
nul homme combien qil fust
present a la journee qui sceust
ne peust ymaginer ne recor
der la verite. Especialement
de la partie des francois tant
y eut poure arroy et petite
ordonnance en leurs grans
convoys qui estoient sans
nombre. Et ce que ie scay
de leurs besoignes z ordon
nances et ce que ie deuse
ray et determineray en ce

taur ie lay sceu et aprins
le plus par moult vaillans
hommes dangleterre saiges
et dyscrets tant chevaliers
comme aultres qui moult
ententifuement auiserent
leur contenant. Et aussi
par les gens de mess. iehan
de haynault qui furent
tousiours delez le roy
phle de france. Cy pse de la
bataille de crecy entre le roy de
france et le roy dangleterre.

biting defeat. For the French wars of the next reign, the English challenged feudal chivalry with infantry and the fire-power of the long-bow.

At Crécy, on 26th August 1346, came the judgment of arms: the English national army of knights, infantry and long-bow men against the chivalry of France and her allies, supported by untrained feudal levies and some bands of mercenaries, including a large body of Genoese cross-bow men. The day began with storms, lightning, and a great flight of crows over the low hills of Ponthieu. When the sun shone, the Genoese stepped warily forward to start the battle, shouting and releasing their bolts, which fell short of the silent English ranks. 'Then the English archers stept forth one pace and let fly their arrows so wholly together and so thick, that it seemed snow.' The Genoese broke and fled, and the French knights rode them down to get at the enemy. And all the while the monotonous hiss of steadily drawn arrows winged into the press of bodies and horses. 'For the bow men let fly among them at large, and did not lose a single shaft, for every arrow told on horse or man, piercing head, or arm, or leg among the riders and sending the horses mad. So the knights in the first French battle fell, slain or sore stricken, almost without seeing the men who slew them.' Even then the deadly surprises were not done, for now the agile English infantry got among the confused knights: 'And also among the Englishmen there were certain rascals that went afoot with great knives, and they went in among the men of arms, and slew and murdered many as they lay on the ground, both earls, barons, knights and squires.'

Feudal military chivalry lay dead, killed by a mere sliver of an arrow and a sneaking knife. The heavy, mounted knight had had his day, to the great woe of those who valued chivalry. The chevalier Bertrand du Guesclin, the image of chivalric virtue, perhaps the best soldier on either side, could not find in the old arrangements of feudalism any answer to the new tactics and national discipline of the English. France did not recover her power until she too learnt to inspire a national army with the fervour of patriotism. The qualities of chivalric knighthood, the qualities of the impetuous, gallant, courteous, quixotic knight-errant, became a lame power, even an embarrassment, in the new warfare. Jacques de Lalaing, the fifteenth-century paragon of the romantic Burgundian court, after vainly seeking the old gallantry of tourneys and noble jousts, of fiery and poetic deeds, died meanly in the real world of western polity, killed at the age of thirty-two in the petty siege of a squalid war, struck by a mangonel shot let off by a frightened boy.

# chapter seven

Chivalry had no cure for the wounds of time. The late Middle Ages were lost in circles more abject, more painful than any Dante saw.

The list of disasters made a doleful record. The realm of faith was shamed by the sins and insolence of the clergy, and broken by the selfish power of kings: the papacy, so exalted by Innocent III, declined from the 'Babylonish captivity' at Avignon to the lower depths of the Great Schism; the papal Curia, composed of suave politicians, degenerated into 'the sink of vice, the sewer of the world'; heresy was more spry than ever, flaunted by Balkan Bogomils, Waldensians of the Alps, Lollards in England, Hussites in Bohemia and Hungary, and by mystical fanatics among the wild-eyed ranks of Spiritual Franciscans, Bégards and Béguins; Christendom itself reeled under the counter-crusade, the *jihad*, of the Turks, which won them Constantinople in 1453, overran Greece and the Balkans, and took them to the gates of Vienna by 1529.

In the world of princes, where morality has at the best a grim hold, there was as much disorder and as much disgrace. Political assassination, a weapon perfected in Italy, became greatly favoured, and regicide a pious duty. In England, Edward II and Richard II both paid in blood for weak character and lackadaisical policy; on the continent, the feud between the House of Orleans and the House of Burgundy was punctuated by alternate murders. The wars of egotism, trade rivalry and dynastic ambition raged on. The dismal episodes of the Hundred Years War exhausted two kingdoms, consumed their revenues and destroyed their people. Kings struggled to extend monarchal control, barons struggled to repossess feudal independence, towns struggled for rights to match their new-found wealth. The poor struggled to remain alive.

The people were inevitably the worst sufferers. For them, the horror of war was hardly more burdensome than the anxiety of peace. Desperation brought on numerous insurrections. The French Jacquerie rose in 1357, followed by their English brethren of the Peasants' Revolt in 1381; throughout the fifteenth century, German peasants and Hussites of the eastern kingdoms, all victims of rural oppression, kept their lands in turmoil. And by way of an ugly jest, a reminder of human insignificance even in the work of destruction, nature sent the affliction of the Black Death, the bubonic plague that swept Europe after 1347, devastating whole countries more thoroughly than the sword had ever done.

What could the weak and misplaced intentions of chivalry do against the irresistible force of a world gone wrong? Chivalric intervention in war or politics only seemed to compound mistakes and hasten failure. The military lesson of Crécy and Poitiers was learnt

The Black Death, 1349: burial of
the plague victims. From the
*Annales de Gilles de Muisit*, 14th
Cent.

reluctantly. At Nicopolis in 1396, the continental cavalry met the
well-drilled Turks of Bayazid II with familiar discord and the old
tactics. Debonair knighthood went down before the disciplined
ferocity of the Janissaries. To flee the field more quickly, the knights
cut the long toes from their pointed shoes. Fifty years later, because
John Hunyadi had broken his truce with the Turks, knighthood
refused its aid to the beleaguered Hungarian champion and watched
his Christian army overwhelmed on the bloody fields of Varna and
Kossovo. And in polity chivalrous judgment was equally unwise.
With excessive generosity, for conspicuous bravery at Poitiers,
Philip, a younger son of the French King, was granted the duchy of
Burgundy in 1363, thus causing a dangerous split in the French domi-
nion, and preparing the way for the great future rivalry between
France and Burgundy.

This age, with man so impotent and life malign, seemed to justify
the laments of the poets. 'Time of sorrow and of temptation,' sighed
Eustache Deschamps, 'age of tears, of envy and of pain.' All mirth
is lost was his message, all hearts have fallen into sadness and despair.
'I, man of sadness,' wrote Chastellain, chronicler of the gorgeous
Burgundian court, 'born in an eclipse of darkness, and thick fogs of
lamentation.' Long gone was the springtime of the troubadours;
pain and grief were the ordinary expectations, and death was a welcome release.

An ideal once fresh and useful, now proved impractical, stiffened
into formality. Chivalry, the high road to noble conduct theoretically

open to every foot, became in failure a tortuous way hedged by regulations, the private path of the well born. As the spirit of knighthood waned, the class of the knights clung more and more to the poor letter of their law; to beat up memories of ancient glory, amid convincing evidence of actual weakness, never were the categories, the nice distinctions, the rules of chivalry more elaborated or more keenly debated.

'To a knight appertaineth that he be lover of the commonweal, for by the commonalty of the people was the chivalry founded and established; and the commonweal is greater and more necessary than any special good.' That admirable statement by Ramon Lull of the democratic foundation of chivalry was slowly modified in the interests of the nobility. When William Caxton came to translate Lull's book, he voiced the general opinion that his words were 'not requisite for every common man to have, but to noble gentlemen that by their virtue intend to come and enter into the noble order of chivalry'. Knights of the late Middle Ages required no popular consensus to confirm them in their place; they were there by right of birth, and chivalry was part of their 'virtue', one of the attributes of their class. A man, in the new age of money, might buy his way into the ranks of chivalry, but the low born could not ascend by grace alone.

Rudimentary instruction prepared the early knight for his life of duty. Fight for God and justice, said the old poems, and you shall not fail. What more was there to add? Be humble, be liberal, 'give largely to all, for the more you give, the more honour you will acquire, and the richer you will be'. That was teaching enough for practical men, living out their ideal in fields of action. But much more was needed to uphold the dignity of a class, to embellish the quality of a noble. The loose admonitions of the early days were exemplified and set down in a rigid code, and young men were taken through this solemn mystery. Since this instruction had in effect no practical value in the great world of war and affairs, it became a ritual initiation into an aristocratic life of fantasy. The ardour of the pursuit was only matched by the fatuity of the accomplishment.

In time of chaos, the nobility looked back to a golden age, seeking in the patterns of chivalry an order and a justification for life. Knowing little of the historical past and quite uncritical in what they knew, liable to take any flight of poetry for sober fact, the nobles conjured from the past a galaxy of mythical heroes, and strove by careful rules to imitate in contemporary courts, where the expense of memorable gestures was most easily borne, the misconceived heroics of a past chivalry. In particular, the four dukes who reigned in Burgundy between 1363 and 1477 promoted a great revival in the formal artifices of chivalry, seeking a resplendence in this display of courtly graces that would make their land the equal of Arthur's fabulous Britain, or at least raise it to the level of the German Empire and the kingdoms of France and England.

The first anxiety in the court of Burgundy was for degrees of rank and niceties of etiquette. The duke himself was so exalted that nothing common or base could come near him; everything he touched, from his sword to his tooth-pick, from the emblems of

*Overleaf, left.* Court feast of the 15th Cent: the cupbearer serves his lord while the court musicians play a sackbut and trumpets from above. Detail from a painting by Wilm Dedeke.

*Overleaf, right.* John the Fearless, Duke of Burgundy. 15th Cent portrait of the Franco-Flemish school.

state to the collar of his hound, was precious and jewelled; and the whole complicated service of his household was designed so that no vulgar or dishonourable act could taint the noble order of his life. The rage for order, as Olivier de la Marche has recorded it, began in the kitchen. Here the chief cook presided in a workaday court that mirrored the proper court upstairs, seated on high and holding the emblem of his office, a big wooden ladle 'which serves a double purpose: on the one hand to taste the broth, on the other hand to harry and chastise the scullions'. Below this formidable figure came his helpers, in a strict hierarchy and with exactly-appointed duties. The keeper of the bread and the cup-bearer were above cook and carver, said de la Marche, because bread and wine became in the sacrifice of the Mass the body and blood of the Saviour, and thus were honoured above all other foods.

Above the kitchens, the rituals increased in awe. The cup-bearer approached with goblet on high, for the duke's wine must not be polluted by lowly breath. At table six doctors attended and advised the duke what to eat, testing for poison with a piece of unicorn's horn. From the table, the duke passed to the functions of state, holding public audience two or three times a week. From a high throne covered with cloth-of-gold, and beneath a canopy of tapestry, the duke gave judgment. Two masters of requests and an *audiencier*, all kneeling before him, handled the petitions, and a clerk, also kneeling, recorded the decisions. The whole court, from princes of the blood to the least squire, had to attend, which they did with patient boredom. Chastellain, who was often there, wrote doubtfully: 'It seemed to be a magnificent and praiseworthy thing, whatever fruit it might bear.' After business, the duke was welcomed by the comforting arms of the court. Forty *valets de chambre* looked after his person. Sixteen picked squires of the best family served him, diverted him, even slept near him. For him they would sing, or play, or recite romances of love and war. For protection, a hundred and twenty-six young men, also of good family, surrounded the duke, and they were assisted by a special body of archers. For his amusement, the duke preferred the solemnity of stately meetings. 'He was in the habit of devoting some part of the day to serious occupations, and, with games and laughter mixed, pleased himself with fine speeches and with exhorting his nobles, like an orator, to practise virtue.'

All virtue flowed from the person of the duke, for the nobles were dependent on him not only for employment and income, but also for the lead in the proper conduct of the chivalrous life. The subtleties of ducal fashion were noted and quickly copied. Gowns were at first long, and then short; hair, on the contrary, was at first short, then long. In 1462 the hair of Duke Philip fell out through disease, and five hundred nobles of the court immediately shaved their heads under the supervision of Pierre de Hagenbach. In time, the vagaries of fashion swung through fantastic excesses. Points of the body, both male and female, were wantonly displayed; doublets became lewdly short while shoes were awkwardly long; outlandish features of Portuguese or English dress, brought over by the foreign consorts

Charles the Bold of Burgundy and his court in council. The Duke wears the device of the Order of the Golden Fleece; the officials of his court, the *audiencier* and clerks, kneel before him. From a manuscript of the late 15th Cent.

of the dukes, were uneasily incorporated without sense or style. In derision at this extravagant bad taste, a certain German prince dressed his jesters in the Burgundian style.

That German cynic was almost alone in his contempt. The grandiose propriety and ceremonial of Burgundy were much admired by the most elegant nobles of Europe, the more so because other courts, especially that of France, the first land of chivalry, were plagued by appalling manners, unseemly breaches of precedence, and even violence. At the coronation feast for Charles VI, in 1380, the Duke of Burgundy had to fight for his rightful place at table; at the funeral of the same king in 1422, the pall-bearers of the coffin came to blows with the monks of Saint-Denis. The coronation feast of Henry VI of England, held in Paris in 1431, was ruined by an uninvited rabble who occupied the tables; and thirty years later Louis XI was harried

Philip the Good of Burgundy in the insignia of the Golden Fleece, the Order of Chivalry he founded on the occasion of his marriage in 1430. From the *Statutes of the Order of the Golden Fleece*, c. 1481.

Young man on horseback: the excesses of aristocratic fashion in the early 15th Cent. From the *Rohan Book of Hours, c.* 1418.

to the very altar of Rheims Cathedral, and the nobility and clergy officiating at the coronation near suffocated by the inquisitive mob.

After such ill-bred disorder, the nobility applauded the punctilious observance of the Burgundians. It was right that John the Fearless knelt to his young daughter-in-law, a princess of France; it was right that Philip the Good instantly raised the siege of Deventer and hurried to Brussels to greet the Dauphin. In 1473, Charles the Bold and the Emperor Frederick III sat in a rain-storm for an hour while they discussed how they should enter Trier, riding side by side as the Emperor wished, or with the Duke modestly behind as Charles insisted. The rights of precedence were debated by the nobility with theological passion and legal ingenuity, and the little competitions in humility were warmly appreciated: the Queen of Spain hides her hand so the young Archduke will not have to kiss it; the young gallant bides his time and in an unguarded moment clutches the royal hand and plants his respect with his lips.

Seeing themselves as the custodians of a delicate art, based on old chivalrous principles, the nobles gathered into 'orders'—distant descendants of Hospitallers and Templars—to preserve their ideal and to announce their exclusivity. The most famous order of the Golden Fleece, founded by Philip the Good on the occasion of his marriage in 1430, was established 'from the great love that we bear to the noble order of chivalry, whose honour and prosperity are our only concern, to the end that the true Catholic faith, the faith of Holy Church, our mother, as well as the peace and welfare of the realm may be defended, preserved and maintained to the glory and praise of Almighty God, and for the furtherance of virtue and good manners'. Pope Eugenius IV welcomed the knights of the Golden Fleece as Maccabeans resurrected, and the twenty-four knightly initiates conducted their affairs with ecclesiastical solemnity and took their vows with religious devotion. A fall from high purpose marked a good name for ever: in the church at Bruges, a black shield above the seat of the Count of Nevers proclaims to this day the shame of his expulsion.

Late chivalry was conscious imitation. 'The high magnificence of heart seen in extraordinary things', the dazzling order of Burgundy in particular, formed but the framework to lives that dared to challenge ancient names. All heroes, imaginary and real, from the archangel Michael to Lancelot of the Lake, from Alexander to that recent brave soldier Bertrand du Guesclin, were elevated into the pantheon of chivalry and given due worship. Hercules was the chief hero-god of Burgundy, his life and deeds set out in a thousand manuscripts, paintings and tapestries. But Hercules alone, insatiate blood-letter that he was, did not exhaust the Burgundian capacity for admiration. The ducal treasury boasted a sword of St George, two swords of du Guesclin, and the tusk of the wild boar that figured in the famous epic *Garin li Loherains*. Charles the Bold, brought up on the deeds of the Arthurian court, set his heart (Chastellain wrote) 'on high and singular purposes for the future and on acquiring glory and renown by extraordinary works'. Commines added that Duke

The Parlement of Charles the Bold, Duke of Burgundy.

Charles plunged into war because he loved Alexander, Hannibal and Caesar best, 'and he longed to resemble those ancient princes become so famous after their death'. The conqueror of Charles, René of Lorraine, knowing he had overcome a worthy opponent, appeared at the Duke's funeral in the long golden beard that ancient victorious heroes had made appropriate for these occasions. Henry V of England, whose active warmongering was commended for keeping 'the discipline of chivalry as it was practised formerly among the Romans', was conducted to his early grave bearing the arms of King Arthur, whose three gold crowns on a blue ground the young dead King had not disgraced.

To be remembered after death and compared in retrospect with ancient heroes was the highest heaven of knightly hopes. Froissart wrote that the French and English champions in the famous Fight of the Thirty set out to 'do so much that people will speak of it in future times in halls, in palaces, in public places, and elsewhere throughout the world'. No knight could expect a happier fate than that of Jacques de Lalaing, celebrated for having been as fair as Paris, as pious as Aeneas, as wise as Ulysses, as brave as Hector.

The virtues that made a knight worthy of posthumous fame were those qualities that this late age thought it perceived in the chivalry of early heroes. The first requirement, universally professed and as generally neglected, was support of the faith and defence of Christen-

dom. Henry V interrupted the service at his death-bed to affirm his crusading intention 'if it had pleased God, his Creator, to let him live to old age'; Philip the Good took a solemn crusading vow in 1454. While princes swore to do their pious duty, the catastrophic ineptitude of western chevaliers at Nicopolis and the relentless Turkish advance afterwards effectively dissuaded them from going further. The bold Duke Philip did little to prevent the loss of Constantinople in 1453, and, despite his vows, he did nothing to attempt its recapture. In the absence of the chivalrous nobility, only a few bands of Italian adventurers came to help the outnumbered Greeks, they alone acting (as one of them proudly said) 'for the honour of God and the honour of all Christendom'.

Best to forget the puzzles of the faith. The second necessity of knightly virtue, an absolute regard for honour, could be approached with more cheerful confidence. 'Death, life, and chivalry are nothing without honour,' wrote one author; 'all is lost without honour', a famous motto added. After King John of France was taken at Poitiers, his son Louis of Anjou went to England as hostage for the captured King. When Anjou dishonourably broke his word and escaped to France, the King was so mortified that he walked immediately into captivity.

The King's action was approved, for honour was the lustre of an individual soul, and took no account of policy. The royal virtue was assured: what did it matter, compared with that, if France lacked a king, or if the royal family had to marry into the dubious ranks of Italian capitalism in order to raise the truly enormous ransom demanded? A knight of Hainault, a vassal of Burgundy, joined the English and was rewarded with the order of the Garter; yet he received great praise from the Burgundian chronicler because he fought bravely to his death and scorned the safety of flight. 'The glory of princes', wrote Chastellain, 'is in their pride and in daring great dangers; all principal powers converge in one small point which is called pride.' Advancing towards Agincourt, Henry V overran the village of his vanguard; but as he was in armour he could not go back, for his own ordinances decreed that a knight dressed for battle could never retreat; the King and a few officers spent an apprehensive night stranded between the armies.

To the pride of kings, a nation's reputation was only a minor tributary of royal honour, and it became a common fiction that matters of state could be settled, and national safety hazarded, by a duel of princes. Richard II proposed to end the outstanding matter between England and France by combat of the royal families. When Richard was done away at Pontefract, Louis of Orleans made himself advocate for the distressed House of York, and challenged the usurper Henry IV to produce the body or fight—'Where is his life? where is his body?' he cried. 'You lie in your false and disloyal throat.' Henry V challenged the French Dauphin before Agincourt, and Philip the Good of Burgundy, that ingenuous chevalier, posted challenges like birthday-gifts. For the future of Holland he challenged Humphrey of Gloucester; for the future of Luxembourg he challenged William of Saxony; and, at last, for the future of Christendom he was ready to do hand-to-hand battle with the Grand Turk himself. Political sense ensured that none of these duels took place. But the challenges seem seriously intended. Duke Philip went into strict training for his fight with Duke Humphrey; he dieted and exercised 'to keep him in breath', and sharpened his sword-play with lessons from the best masters; the lists were built, the splendid armour prepared, the banners sewn, the heralds instructed. Nor can it be said that his motives were unworthy. 'To prevent Christian bloodshed and the destruction of the people for whom my heart has compassion', he intended to settle this quarrel 'by my own body, without going as far as war, which would condemn many noblemen and others, both yours and mine, to end their days piteously'.

The truly honourable man, prince or knight, would show the quality of a *prudhomme*, a difficult term that each age took in its own way. It meant, perhaps, the imitation of the good action of a hero. Roland and Oliver were *prudhommes*, so in fiction were the Alexander of the romances, Lancelot, Gawain and the warriors of the Round Table, so too in fact were Godfrey of Bouillon, St Louis and his good servant Joinville. The *prudhomme* was not just the man of heroic force; for such a one, for a Richard Lionheart, the term was *preux*. But the more honourable man had within him the infusion of Christian chivalry. Philip Augustus, grandfather of St

Du Guesclin invested with the sword of the Constable of France by King Charles V. From a 15th Cent manuscript.

Louis, used to explain that the prowess of the *prudhomme* was in the service of God, and was nothing less than a direct gift from God.

The early knight proved himself *prudhomme* by humble dedication of his power to God and Church and people. The later knight showed himself *prudhomme* by jealous guardianship of his pride and his place. Something of the difference may be seen in those innocent moments of conversation between saintly king and honest vassal that make Joinville's *Life of St Louis* so endearing. Joinville, who had once told the King that he would rather commit thirty mortal sins than be a leper, though the King reproved him, for there was 'no leprosy as ugly as mortal sin', disappointed the King further by his uncharitable pride: 'He asked me if I washed the feet of the poor on Maundy Thursday. "God forbid, sir!" I answered. "No, I will not wash the feet of these brutes!" "In truth," he said, "that was a poor reply; you should not despise what God did as a lesson to us. I pray you then, first for God's sake and then for mine, make it your habit to wash them."' Joinville's faith absolutely forbade him to break his oath, yet his nobility despised Christ's poor. St Louis, the rigorous Christian visionary, was the old *prudhomme*. Honest Joinville, punctilious aristocrat, was among the first of the new.

'Honour', wrote the Burgundian chronicler Chastellain, 'urges every noble nature to love all that is noble in his being.' Knights of the later chivalry became *prudhommes* only by a perpetual and wary contemplation of what was due from, and due to, their pride and rank. Old chivalry took free and appropriate action under the large vows of service to God and country; new chivalry was a strict prisoner to the tyranny of rules, oaths, gestures. At Caesarea, Joinville threatened to leave the army because a royal man-at-arms had pushed one of his knights. The offender had to come barefoot and in small-clothes, with naked sword, offering his hands to be cut off, before the insult was wiped out. In the Hundred Years War four knights, rushing with vital dispatches, pulled up dumbfound at the general's horse, for none knew which one had the right to speak first. In the same war, Froissart saw an Englishman fight with an eye covered, for he had sworn to use only one eye until his reputation was made. He was not unusual. The fine soldier du Guesclin would not undress until he had taken Montcontour, and on other occasions put his success in jeopardy by the impracticability of his vows. A Pole won great acclaim by an oath, which he kept for nine years, only to eat and drink standing. Jean de Bourbon and sixteen companions vowed to wear fetters each Sunday—gold for knights, silver for squires—until an equal number of opponents could be induced to do battle with them.

Joinville thought the only proper fight was one between equally matched knights, with no 'shooting of arrows or bolts'. Jean de Beaumont considered it wrong and dishonourable of the French to use the levies of the Paris guilds at Agincourt, for the French would then outnumber the English three to one. Such attitudes deserved the defeat they invited. At Najera, in 1367, Henry of Trastamara, anxious for a fair fight, came down from his advantageous position, and was drubbed by the Black Prince for his courtesy. At Nicopolis, in 1396, the French knights demanded that their nobility should give them the first line of battle, though the King of Hungary begged them to allow the seasoned troops in that place. The French won their point, but lost disastrously to the Turks.

Obviously, to hold to such folly put battles and armies and countries in danger. So those warriors who professed this chivalry most ardently had to learn painfully not to practise it. Froissart recorded the mixed admiration at the Fight of the Thirty, the duel of French and English companies that bloodied a Breton field in 1351: 'Some held it a prowess, and some held it a shame and a great overbearing.' Duels were thereafter regarded with suspicion; Guy de la Trémoïlle was not permitted to prove French superiority in single combat. Duels stole another's honour and won only vainglory; they squandered money and distracted from the proper conduct of a war. Even Philip the Good gave up the pretence of chivalry on the field of battle, and learnt the greater power of strategy and cunning. In one day he avoided the enemy three times, and he allowed a decoy to wear his own magnificently conspicuous armour.

The knight's greatest happiness was still, as always, the joy of warfare. Never was he so alive, so completely a man, as on the battlefield. 'You love your comrades so in war,' said the *Jouvencel*, the account of the exploits of Jean de Bueil. 'When you see that your quarrel is just and your blood is fighting well, tears rise to your eyes. Sweet feelings of loyalty and pity fill your heart when you see your friend so valiantly expose his body, exercising his manhood as our Creator intended. Then you strive to live or die with him, and for love never to desert him. And from this there arises such a joy that he who has tasted it cannot even express his delight. Does such a man fear death? Not at all, for he is so strengthened, so elated, he forgets himself entirely.'

But the changing nature of warfare, to which the gallant misconceptions of chivalry could not adapt, dimished the artless joy of the fighting noble. No longer did he find the bracing clash of knights, settling great matters without the interference of profane hands, uncleansed by chivalry. War was now a ruinous affair ruled by dishonour. Sinister participants held the field: the free companies, that 'great number of pillagers and robbers' (Froissart complained) 'who said they must needs live'; *routiers* like Sir John Hawkwood, 'a knight right hardy and of great experience', one also available to the best offer and not particular in his methods of war; sullen townsmen and uprooted peasants with a vindictive hatred for their noble oppressors. Denied the convenient ransom or clean sword-stroke, the knight awaited an agonizing and demeaning death, seeing the sky darken with arrows, facing a thickset hedge of pike and spear, overwhelmed by the vengeful spite of a vulgar militia.

The most famous knights of the late Middle Ages expended their lives in pitiful impotence, lost figures in a forlorn world. The renowned Marshal Boucicaut trailed his high bravery from defeat to defeat, from Nicopolis to Agincourt, and died in miserable captivity. Jacques de Lalaing, mirror of courtly virtue, agitated a dozen courts with futile search for heroic deeds. He achieved nothing—not a battle won by his presence, not a tyrant put down, not a maiden rescued. At his death, in 1453, he left the draft of a challenge which revealed the extent of his schoolboy ambition. He dared any nobleman, who would prevent him taking a goblet from the German Emperor's table, stand against him in the lists and fight for that goblet. Jean de Bueil, who had fought the bitter campaign under Joan of Arc, was disgraced by the King. In retirement, he told the real tale of war. He spoke of the pains and the ironies, of knights reduced to spavined unshod horses, of battles done by lame and one-eyed men, of clothes-stores raided to patch the ragged captain's shirt, of pillagers content with one lean cow.

Olivier de la Marche, chronicler of the Burgundian court, deeply mourned the death of Lalaing, flower of chivalry, cut down in his

Joan of Arc, from the *Lives of Famous Women, c.* 1500.

early prime. 'The renown of the virtues, disposition, and chivalry of Lalaing', he proclaimed, 'will be perpetuated not only by his contemporaries and in their memories, but also as long as writings exist in the world.' The wondrous chevalier is completely forgotten. How galling for the chivalrous chronicler had he known that the genius of the age, the person universally celebrated for political and military wisdom, and also for something superhuman beyond those, was de Bueil's humble general, the untutored Joan of Arc, a peasant, and a woman to boot.

From the brutal indifference of the real world, chivalry retreated into fantasy, guiding itself by the simplified forms of ideal conduct as they appeared in the literature of romance. In the circle of the court, safe from the oppression of vulgar events, knighthood played out its dream of the courtly life.

Since he had stumbled in war, and since pride still demanded the use of arms and the proof of valour, the knight turned with a new passion to the formal contest of joust and tourney. And nowhere handled these shows with greater dexterity or more grandeur than the court of Burgundy. The Church still condemned the waste and the danger, though in Burgundy, out of deference to the duke, clerics sat with spectators and the Bishop of Langres appeared in a jouster's retinue. Townsmen and poets mocked the 'idiocy and folly' of the entertainment, 'the pride of heart and vainglory' of the combatants. Whenever did Cicero or Scipio joust, Petrarch indignantly asked? But to men like Lalaing the joust was the salt of existence, and knights from the corners of Europe came gladly to Burgundy for the honour and the financial rewards of the great tournaments, and their deeds were the stuff of honourable history. 'It would be a sad pity and loss', wrote Olivier de la Marche, 'if such assaults-at-arms were passed over in silence or forgotten.' If he did so he would be failing in his duty as an historian.

Each tournament was a piece of artistry, a magnificent fiction conceived in high romantic style. Each boldly invited comparison with the episodes of King Arthur and the adventures of the Round Table. Fictional dragons were slain, fictional maidens rescued, fictional ogres done to death. The passage of arms took place at 'The tree of Charlemagne', or 'The fountain of tears', or 'The tree of gold'. Extravagant allegorical representations set the scene; giants, dwarves, rare animals, grotesques of all kinds brought it to life; princes and noble contestants solemnly took their places in the living picture. For the jubilee year 1450, Philip the Good sent his ace Lalaing to Chalon, to organize and maintain the *Pas de la Fontaine aux Pleurs* for the whole twelve months, knowing well that knights from all northern Europe would pass through the town on their pilgrimage to Rome. On an island in the Sâone, Lalaing set up a sumptuous pavilion, in which the image of a weeping woman hung beneath a Madonna, the tears flowing into a basin held by a unicorn, who also bore three shields speckled with blue tears. Those who sought to rescue the 'Lady of the Fountain of Tears' from her mysterious but steadfast grief advanced and struck one of the shields, the white shield if he wished to fight with the axe, the violet one

*Overleaf.* The showing of the helms before a tournament. From the *Livre des Tournois du Roi René*, *c.* 1460.

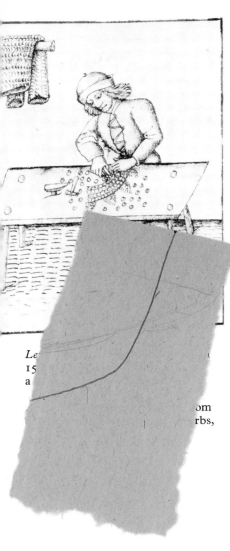

to fight with the sword, and the black one for combat with horse and lance. For a year the jousts continued under the judgment of the King-at-Arms of the Golden Fleece. Those beaten in the lists received a golden bracelet, which they must wear for a year, unless some kind lady would unlock it and claim the services of the prisoner. The champions received from Lalaing axe, sword, or lance, all of gold. Feasts and entertainments beguiled the time not spent in fighting, and the whole glorious business was brought to a fitting close with a banquet in honour of the ladies of Chalon.

Invention strained for rich and exotic effects. Claude de Vaudrey, in quest of the Savage Lady at the *Pas de la Dame Sauvage*, having wandered in pretence through the solitary land of *Pensées* and the bog of *Imagination*, arrived at the lists with an entourage of naked servants, savage men with trumpets and banners leading savage women on horseback, hiding their lasciviousness with long golden hair. At the *Emprise du dragon*, in honour of Margaret of Anjou at her departure for England, four knights at a cross-roads detained every lady until some noble jouster redeemed her in battle. At the same entertainment, foreboding the tragic fate of his daughter, King René was dressed all in black, and black too were his horse, his harness, his weapons, even to the wood of his lance.

How well these tourneys of love and prowess illuminated a drab life. The town was hectic with activity; armourers, harness-makers, saddlers, farriers, goldsmiths, silversmiths, embroiderers, carpenters, grooms, all worked until hands and backs ached, and so too did the pot-boys, tavern-keepers, rhymesters, whores and pickpockets. Round the palace foamed the haughty tide of nobles, pricking mettlesome horses into nervous action. The crowd reined back with false respect, jeering and cheering, eyeing the champions like bulls in a ring, judging the power of the arm, the weight of battle-axe or mace, putting money on some resplendent giant, some lithe young cavalier, some grim-faced wildman from the distant border-lands. In casual disarray, with unfitted armour strewn around, the jousters lord it in their open tents with the *banderoles* (the 'colours') on their arms. The ring of brass, loudly aided by the racket of kettle-drums, destroys all peace. Frenzy mounts to that golden moment, when the duke steps out in the summer morning, and the first blows crash down.

No occasion was more fit for show than the marriage of a duke of Burgundy. No duke received worthier entertainment than Charles the Bold when he married Margaret of York at Bruges on 3rd July 1468. The fiction had been long prepared: Anthony, the Great Bastard of Burgundy, half-brother of the Duke, would hold the *Arbre d'Or* against all-comers. The Lady of the 'hidden isle' had entreated the Bastard, for love of her, to undertake a hundred and one passes with the lance, a hundred and one passes with the sword, and to decorate the Golden Tree with the arms of mighty champions.

The Mass was done, the procession ushered to the barriers of the market-place by the Bastard's trumpeters, in scarlet livery adorned with the golden tree. Cheering populace packed the tribunes. The ladies, somewhat fatigued by the rigours of the entry, had changed

*Left.* Tournament in honour of Queen Jane, wife of Henry IV of England. The arrangement of the lists is clearly seen, with the barrier separating the charging jousters, and the pages and supernumeraries in attendance. From the Pageants of Richard Beauchamp, Earl of Warwick, *c.* 1493.

*Above.* A tournament in honour of Charles VIII: the entry of a champion into the lists. From the *Livre des Tournois du Roi René, c.* 1460.

their dress and now fanned themselves in the stand opposite the gilded trunk of the Golden Tree. The Duke shone in gold embroidery trimmed with marten fur; the Duchess was in crimson and gold brocade edged with ermine. Round about, the nobles vied in splendour and ostentation. Silks, satins, damasks, taffetas, rich furs, in a wonder of artful styles, flashed on every side; feathers, plumes, cockades and strange devices waved from the heads; the Bastard Baldwin flew a long green sash from his helmet, while the Count of Salm crowned his armour with a lady's head-piece. But all was changed at the day's end, and the sport next morning enlivened with a new display of peacock-colours.

The dwarf on a platform turned the hour-glass, blew the signal on his horn, and the knights advanced to the lists, presenting themselves with whatever daring or foolish ingenuity they could devise. A mishap denied the Bastard Anthony his full measure of glory: a horse had kicked him on the knee, and his place in the lists was taken by the young Lord Scales, opening the tournament against Lord Ravenstein, whose decrepit age gave him the honour of the first pass. But no injury could be allowed to dull the high festivity. Anthony performed his administrative functions lolling in a luxurious carriage, as if he were 'not a Bastard of Burgundy, but the heir of one of the greatest rulers in the world'. And for nine days the spectacle

203

continued until Duke Charles himself advanced to the lists, led
forward by the state trumpeters and bandsmen, the King-at-Arms
of the Golden Fleece, the officers, heralds and noblemen of the household, pages, servants and the state horses. The hour-glass turned for
the last time; the opponent, once more the Duke's cousin Lord
Ravenstein, awaited. Nineteen lances were broken, and the jousts
were at an end.

After the jousts came the tourney between knights split into opposing companies, all dressed in violet velvet, all armed with lance and sword. This was the most ancient and barbarous part of the tournament, the violent opposition of war-bands:

Now ringen trumpets loud and clarion;
There is no more to say, but west and east
In go the spears full sadly in arrest;
In goeth the sharp spur into the side.
There men see who can joust and who can ride;
There shivered shafts upon shields thick;
He feeleth through the heart's-bone the prick.
Up springen spears twenty foot in height;
Out go the swords as the silver bright.

Chaucer knew very well not only the brilliance of the tourney, but the hurt and danger too: 'Out broke the blood, with stern streams red.' So it happened that summer day in Bruges. The Duchess, fearing for the life of her lord, gave the signal to stop; the dwarf blew his horn until his cheeks cracked; the ladies fluttered veils in dismay. But the fury did not abate until the Duke went among the fighters, not as a jouster but as a ruler, and knocked noble heads indiscriminately, 'sparing none, whether he were cousin, English-man or Burgundian'. After the vigour of the field, the banquet reconciled all passions. John Wydeville, brother of the English Queen, was tactfully declared the victor. A largesse of six hundred francs was distributed to the servants of the tourney, and the great affair closed to the blaring of trumpets.

Great events required noble celebration, and the nuptials of Charles and Margaret, which the English gentleman John Paston witnessed with awe, maintained the standards of opulence that Philip the Good had set for the court. A special building, 140 feet long, 70 wide and over 60 high, was constructed in Brussels and shipped to Bruges. The ceiling was lined with blue and white woollen cloth, the walls decked with tapestries and cloth-of-gold. This great hall contained elaborate castles in which men lurked working the machinery of the pantomime, artificial rocks which some scaled, and thickets of greenery complete with wild animals. From the moment Margaret landed in Sluys, on 25th June 1468, until 10th July, a week after the wedding day, the pace of the entertainment did not let up; processions, allegories, pantomimes, jousts, feasts, musical offerings followed each other with dizzy speed, with more energy than taste. Among the surprising constructions were a singing lion and singing asses, whistling goats and tuneful wolves, wooden elephants, camels, unicorns and a dragon belching flames. A whale opened to reveal knights and sirens. The presiding effigy, symbolic of the union, was the Burgundian unicorn mounted by the English leopard who held in one paw the standard of England, and in the other paw a marguerite. 'As for the Duke's court,' John Paston surmised, 'as of lords, ladies and gentlewomen, knights, squires and gentlemen, I heard never of none like to it, save King Arthur's court.' If that were so, then the dearest intention of the dukes of Burgundy was realized.

But the pursuit of romantic grandeur served for more than amuse-

A tournament conducted before King Arthur: jousters were offered a choice of weapons, and though the contest between mounted knights with the lance was the most exacting discipline, contests with sword, axe, or club, mounted or on foot, were also popular. From *Guiron*, late 15th Cent.

206

ment. The prince of high chivalry, especially in Burgundy, ruled by noble gesture, giving the ordinary decisions of state politics a mystery and elegance that overawed opposition. Policy, as well as entertainment, followed the model of romance, bound by such strange ritual as the poets described. In the French poem *The Vow of the Heron*, the English court persuade Edward III to embark on the Hundred Years War by undergoing a series of ferocious oaths. The pregnant Queen herself vows to give birth only in the land of the enemy, and to kill herself if the King has made no move by the time of her delivery.

When Constantinople, the grandest city of Christiandom, fell to the Turks in May 1453, Philip the Good saw that some extraordinary action was needed, and clearly such action could not be set afoot without a most solemn and chivalrous commitment. To promote a crusade which never left, he held at Lille, on 17th February 1454, the Oath of the Pheasant. Here men, animals and machinery competed in a lively but confused symbolism. Among the representations described by Olivier de la Marche were the statue of a naked child that '*pissoit eau rose continuellement*'; a pie that enclosed twenty-four musicians performing hollowly beneath the pastry; a fool mounted on a bear among icicle-covered crags; an Indian forest patrolled by clockwork animals; two pillars, one adorned with a half-naked lady representing Constantinople, and the other with a lion representing the Duke of Burgundy. These allegories were merely the preparation. After the feast, a turbaned Moorish giant approached leading an elephant. From the back of the beast a damsel representing the Church (la Marche himself in unlikely disguise) implored the aid of Burgundy in long rhetorical verse. Now the officers of the Golden Fleece advanced to take the vows of the court: 'The King-at-Arms bore a live pheasant, decorated with a collar of gold and precious stones. Approaching the Duke, he made a profound obeisance, and said, that it being the custom at grand festivals to offer to the prince and gentlemen a peacock, or some noble bird, for them to make a vow upon, he had come with two ladies to offer to his valour a pheasant.' Then the Duke made his vow, to follow his lord paramount or any other prince on crusade, and if need be to fight hand-to-hand with the Grand Turk. After Duke Philip, the nobles came forward, each with some extravagant or preposterous resolution: to wear no armour until the Turks are checked; to stand up to meals; to abstain from wine; to wear a hair-shirt; to sleep on the floor every Saturday night. In a questionable spirit of mockery one fellow swore to possess his mistress before he left for the crusade: or else to marry the first heiress he met with twenty thousand crowns. Thus by a kind of specious magic Constantinople was as good as recaptured, and the deficiencies of knighthood glossed over.

After the maintenance of honour, nothing in the canons of chivalry was more important than the rites of courtesy. In the mythology of the court, the lady sanctified all with her kind eyes, and the knight moved heaven and earth to live even in the shadow of her smile. 'Love', said the *Mémoirs de Boucicaut*, 'obliterates all pain and lightens

A feast, from a Flemish manuscript of the 15th Cent: Miracles de Notre-Dame, illustrated by Jean Tavernier for Philip the Good.

all burdens borne for the beloved.' The father of Jacques de Lalaing instructed him 'that few gentle men come to high estate of prowess and good renown, save if they have some lady or damosel of whom they are amorous; but take heed my son, that it be not light love, for so should you be forever held in great villainy and reproach.' The powerfully amorous eyes of Philip the Good, which (wrote Chastellain) 'looked on men as fiercely as a lion', inclined benignly on the ladies. A certain knight attended the tourney of the *Arbre d'Or* in the guise of a slave, to announce his despairing service of a cold lady.

But in the matter of courtesy, as in so much else, the practice was a stranger to the theory. Princes had mistresses as they had always done, such gallantry being accounted part of the adulterous courtly tradition. Philip the Good in particular was respected for the healthy state of his sexual appetite and the legion of his bastards. Yet by all the rules the nip of lust could never excuse discourtesy, vulgarity or crudity. These marks of shame, however, were too easily apparent in every court. The court of mad King Charles VI of France and Queen Elizabeth was rent by scandal, lechery, meanness and squalor. The Queen loathed the sick King and would not approach his suppurating and vermin-ridden body. The King hated the Queen and would strike her and her Bavarian attendants in his rage. The royal children were utterly neglected, the Dauphin complaining that his mother had not caressed him in three months. The King took his mistress and the Queen plunged into frivolity, expense and perhaps adultery with her own brother-in-law. The people, shouting abuse at her flaccid body and gross breasts, were led away to the hangman: 'Go about in disguise and you wiil soon hear what is spoken of you,' a preacher told the Queen. 'Lady Venus wields the sceptre at your court; drunkeness and dissipation are her companions.'

The court of Charles VII was little better. Agnès Sorel, the low-born mistress, tyrannized Queen and courtiers with her brazen effrontery, wanton, mincing, rouged and painted, with shoulders and breasts bare, with head-dress higher and train longer than any poor Queen Marie wore. The mistress usurped the Queen's estate and received the homage of nobles, even visiting princes, with the pride of an empress. The blasphemous end of her presumption was to be painted as a lewd Madonna for the Church of Notre-Dame in Melun. Philip the Good, as befitted a duke of Burgundy, was discreet and dignified in his many amours, but it was a strange notion of courtesy to provide an expensive brothel for an English embassy—noble men bound by their code to noble ladies. Yet for them and their retinue, Chastellain tells us, 'baths were provided with everything required for the calling of Venus, to take by choice and election what they liked best, and all at the expense of the Duke'. And with far greater stain on his honour and courtesy Duke Philip handed Joan of Arc to the English. No doubt it was intolerable for any knight, in particular a prince of chivalry, to consider how much this ignorant girl had wrought alone, where all the chevaliers had failed.

*Opposite, top.* The galleys of the Western armies at Nicopolis, 1396. The brave but inept conduct of Western chivalry at Nicopolis hopelessly failed to stop the Turkish advance towards western Europe. From a 15th Cent manuscript of the *Chroniques de Froissart.*

*Opposite, bottom.* A feast, from the *Grand Alexandre,* 15th Cent.

Far from being a figure for veneration, women had become in practice an object for sexual use. There were said to be three thousand whores in Paris, a bold army of gilded rogues quite beyond the control of the authorities. They prospered because they answered the clamourings of male lust. It was held against Charles the Bold that, among other failings, he was chaste. The rank corruption of ungoverned lust, the sweaty ferment of constant rutting, so nauseated the moralists that they blasted womankind with sole responsibility for the sins of debased courtesy.

Medieval woman as sexual object. Debauchery at the baths.

*Right*. Venus and her children: a 15th Cent illustration for 'The Franklin's Tale' in Chaucer's *Canterbury Tales*.

*Overleaf, left*. Portrait of Charles the Bold, Duke of Burgundy.

*Overleaf, bottom right*. Knights of the 15th Cent attack the infidel. Detail of a votary painting, *c.* 1450.

*Overleaf, top right*. A tourney, from the *Grand Alexandre*, 15th Cent.

If blame there were, it lay elsewhere, resting chiefly on the shoulders of the two poets who compiled the *Roman de la Rose*. This long poem, as influential as any in western history, was the presentation of two kinds of love. In the pastoral allegories of the first section of the poem, written by Guillaume de Lorris about the year 1240, men discovered a formal exposition of the courtly code. The lover enters the sweet mysteries of the Garden of Love, led on by the god Amor with all the good virtues dancing attendance. The instruction of the god makes the seeker worthy: 'Whoever wants Love to be his lord, courteous and without pride must be, elegant and affable, and

The meeting of the lovers in the Rose Garden. From a 14th Cent. Ivory plaque.

endowed with generosity.' Though threatened by Slander, Fear and Shame, and the ugly ranks of their guilty cohorts, the lover advances to pluck the rose. But before his purified hands can touch the object of his desire, the poem breaks off.

The completion of the poem, written by Jean de Meung some forty years later, descended from the Arcadian ideal into a vigorous cynicism. The poet explains at great length, with many digressions and sly stories, by what hypocritical tricks the rose may be plucked. The poem was a textbook for seduction, a pander to sensuality, composed in clinical detail, and with a sure knowledge of sexual pathology. Virginity is the way to hell: to Jean de Meung, women are wantons all, with more seamy arts than day can reveal, and every man is a satyr below the waist.

The *Roman de la Rose* was universally read, discussed, copied, and translated, Chaucer himself giving us an English version. The striking realism of de Meung, showing so well the weakness and desires of humans, had the greater fame and effect. Women were hotly pursued, and, as an ironic consequence, as hotly abused. The invective of Francois Villon, and others less famous but more important in their day, condemned women for bringing on this riot of the flesh. Almost alone, Christine de Pisan fought the male

*Above.* Courtly diversions: the round dance. From the *Roman de la Rose*, 15th Cent.

*Overleaf, left.* Development of chivalric mythology: ladies, knights and dragons. From the Breviary of the Duke of Bedford, 1425.

*Overleaf, top right.* The Renaissance hunt of the Emperor Charles V, by Cranach.

*Overleaf, bottom right.* 'A mon seul desir': the lady is about to retire to the pavilion, to dress herself in the presents of the beloved, and to await his arrival; the lion symbolizes the bridegroom, and the unicorn the bride. From the last of a set of six tapestries of the 15th Cent, most probably intended as a betrothal gift.

conspiracy, and upheld the name of women against de Meung and his vast company of supporters.

But Guillaume de Lorris was not without followers. The way he proposed through the Garden of Love was the path of courtly courtesy. These nobles who revolted against, but could not change, the onslaught on sensuality, discovered in the aristocratic refinement and the gentle, other-worldly topography of the Garden a spur for a flight into formalized fantasy. They employed, in effect, the usual method whereby chivalry blinded its eyes to reality. That man of dreams Marshal Boucicaut founded the order of 'the green shield for fair ladies' to protect all women, but more especially widows. When asked once why he respectfully saluted some Genoan whores, the Marshal replied, so pure was his courtesy, that he would 'rather do reverence to ten whores than to fail in respect to one woman'. The lead of the Marshal was naturally followed by the court of Burgundy. In 1401 Philip the Bold, the first of the four great dukes, founded a *cours amoureuse*, partly for entertainment during a plague (obviously following the model of the *Decameron*), and partly to encourage, by debate and precept, the courtly devotion due to the lady.

In the high region of hot air into which these discussions ascended,

Silene.

Que queris hic Holanis.

pumris hic aduemsti: vel quo
nomine vocteris. Sanctus ge
orgius dixit. Xpianus ⁊ dei
seruus sum: georgius nuncu
por genere capadocis pūe mee
comitatum gerens. Elegi vero
temporali carere diguitate: et

imortalis dei umpio deseruire. se ūj
actanus dixit. Eras
georgi: accede ⁊ un
molta deo apollim.
Leatus georgius respondit. Do
mino iesu xpisto exhibeo cultu
ram omniū seculor: non appol

love became, like other aspects of outmoded chivalry, a complex affair of signs, gestures and rules. There was a language of courtly love in which the symbols were jewels, colours, flowers. When the poet Machaut saw his beloved for the first time, he rejoiced that she was wearing a white dress with a blue hood on which there was a design of green parrots, for green signified new love and blue fidelity. There were games and conundrums of love, all of which were resolved only by the application of very strict rules. In the account that the aged and gouty poet Machaut left of his romantic love for the beautiful young Péronelle d'Armentières, the steps of his wooing were both strictly correct and mildly salacious. A kiss might be snatched, some blissful moments spent lying next his beloved, just so long as the forms of propriety were observed. Reputation came before virtue. Having worshipped Péronelle with all the old courtly confusion between beloved and goddess, Machaut, a Canon of Rheims, sadly saw her go, but resolved to consecrate his heart to her memory alone, and to pray God to record her name in the blessed roll of heaven.

History deals harshly with the late medieval knight: a beast in the world, a fool at court. Certainly the conventions of late chivalry make him a preposterous figure, a slave to pride and artifice and sentimentality. Perhaps in his ordinary moments he was not so very strange, just a familiar human subject to familiar passions. Occasionally in the literature, amid the rhetoric and the bluster, the humanity shows, as it did when Jean de Beaumont speaks in *The Vow of the Heron*: 'When we are in the tavern, drinking strong wines, and the ladies pass and look at us, with those white throats and tight bodices, those sparkling eyes of smiling beauty, then nature makes the heart desire, and then we could conquer Yaumont and Agoulant, Roland and Oliver. But when we are in camp on our charging horses, with shields round our necks and our lances lowered, and the great cold is congealing us together, and our limbs are crushed before and behind, and our enemy looms near, then we wish to be hidden in a cellar so large that no one could ever see us.'

# chapter eight

*Above.* The childhood of the knight: children at play, from *Romans de Chevalerie, c.* 1280.

*Below, right.* The childhood of the knight: swimming, from *Vie de St Denis.*

*Overleaf, left.* The Gate of Hell, with the seven deadly sins listed below. From the *Book of Hours* of Catherine of Cleves, 1435.

*Overleaf, top right.* The romantic image: knight on a flowered ground. From a 15th Cent tapestry.

The fallen rose in triumph. Having passed from useful practice to barren formality, and finally divorced from the tears and faults of the dying feudal world, chivalry entered at last into the realm of the imagination, where true power lies. The familiar forces of our day are but the reverberations of ancient theory; the failed hopes of wandering knights have bequeathed the west two of its strongest and most enduring concepts. The idea of the gentleman and the religion of romantic love are both legacies of fighting horsemen.

What began as a desperate stratagem to correct brutal, irresponsible power became in time a system of ethics. John of Salisbury, the kindliest thinker of the high days of knighthood, looked on chivalry as a way to purify the State, to make men moral and peaceful and upright. Others of optimistic or enthusiastic nature agreed.

'Two things', said *Le Livre des faicts de Boucicaut*, 'have, by the will of God, been established in the world, like two pillars to sustain the divine and human laws, without which the world would be mere confusion and disorder, and these two flawless pillars are Chivalry and Learning, which go very well together.' In chivalry were the seeds of a better world. It was the duty of all teachers to plant those seeds, and to nourish the growth by making universally known the true art of chivalrous living.

Instruction was at first by precept and example within the family of knighthood, the young aspirant being sent, at about the age of twelve, to become a page and then a squire in some noble household, and there he served the apprenticeship of chivalry. The lessons were chiefly of a practical kind to prepare for the active life. An English document listed the essential accomplishments: riding, boxing, archery, swimming, hunting, chess-playing, and making verses. At the age of thirteen, Little John, page at the French court and the young hero of the late medieval *Le Petit Jehan de Saintré*, was already 'skilful and hardy' at riding an unbridled horse, at singing, dancing, playing tennis, running and leaping, and it was time for the fair lady who had befriended him to teach him something of morals

and manners. Be religious, sober, temperate, peaceful and truthful, she admonished him: 'Likewise be loyal of hands and mouth, and serve every man as best you may. Seek the fellowship of good men; hearken to their words and remember them. Be humble and courteous wherever you go, boasting not nor talking overmuch, neither be dumb altogether. Look to it that no lady or damosel be in reproach through your default, nor any woman of whatsoever quality. And if you fall into company where men speak disworshipfully of any woman, show by gracious words that it pleaseth you not, and depart.'

Courtly conventions in romantic literature: court ball for the betrothal of Clarisse de Gascogne with Renaud de Montauban. From a 15th Cent manuscript.

And to sweeten this worthy moral instruction the lady also taught her young servitor the arts of elegance beloved of gentlemen, and sent him off with a purse to buy the finery that would make him fit for a lady's regard: a doublet of crimson damask or satin; two pairs of good hose, one of fine scarlet and the other of Saint-Lô brunet, embroidered down the side with a lady's device; four pairs of fine linen shirts and four kerchiefs; well-made slippers and shoes. A dashing figure, it was hinted, might lead to tantalizing rewards. 'I shall,'

Lancelot and Queen Guinevere.

the lady promised, 'God willing, soon do more for you.'

An active, virtuous body, loyal and courteous, was the main end of chivalric education; a heroic figure in elegant rig was more prized than powers of the mind. A knight was expected to know enough to show himself easy and affable on all occasions, and to bear his part among the civilized diversions of the court. If he were to study, his best guide was history, either the history of fact or the history of romance (the two were hardly separated), and to find in the real or

*Right.* Two lovers, *c.* 1480.

*Below.* The awakening of the knight and the reading of the inscription on the magic fountain. From the *Livre du Cuer d'Amour espris* by René d'Anjou, 1455.

*Opposite.* The pleasures of the hunt. From the *Legende des Klosters Polling*.

fictional past the exemplars for the good life. 'So,' said the lady to Little John, 'by thus reading, hearkening to and remembering noble histories, ensamples and teachings, you may acquire the everlasting joys of Paradise, honour in arms, honour in wisdom and honour in riches, and live worshipfully and cheerfully.' But his inquiries did not have to be profound or far-reaching. That ideal knight Jacques de Lalaing had the schooling considered best for gentlemen which, said the chronicle of his life, 'in a passing short time made him expert and well able to speak, understand, and write in Latin and in French; taught him how to hunt and hawk so that none excelled him; how to play chess, backgammon and other gentlemanly sports as well as any man of his age, for truth to tell, God and nature had forgot nothing in the making of him'.

Instruction within the household was at best a haphazard way to teach chivalry, for the household was governed by the whim of the lord, and the lord himself was at the mercy of events. Enthusiasts of chivalry saw the need for a steadier method. Ramon Lull, at the end of the thirteenth century, pleaded for schools or academies of chivalry; his two translators Sir Gilbert Hay and William Caxton, living in the severe chaos of the breakdown of feudalism, supported Lull's argument. No academies were established, which was perhaps as well, since chivalry was more a preparation for practical virtue than a narrow subject for the schools. But when strong monarchs resolved the worst part of national discord, swept away feudalism, and founded the large courts that gave each nation a centre for both government and culture, the powerful court also became the central household for all the nobility, and young men who in former ages would have learnt their chivalry in a hundred dangerous places up and down the land, now made their way to the capital and studied the qualities of a gentleman under the grand and steady patronage of the king.

The training given in the new Renaissance courts hardly differed from the one that Lull had advocated, that *Le Petit Jehan* had taught, or that Lalaing had received. There was more learning, for the new age was enthusiastic about scholarship, but there was the same insistence on prowess, exercise, elegance, manners, and recreation. These were the true grounds for chivalric excellence that Castiglione set out with such authority and such lasting effect in his famous book *Il Cortegiano*, which Sir Thomas Hoby translated into English in 1561.

To the new thinking it was no longer excusable even for the soldier (which the courtier was at heart) to be ignorant. 'I hold opinion', said the authority of Castiglione, 'that it is not so necessary for any man to be learned, as it is for a man of war.' A courtier must have knowledge in order to speak and write well, and to gain this Castiglione would set him at 'those studies, which they call humanity, and to have not only understanding of the Latin tongue, but also of the Greek'. But ancient learning was only the beginning of knowledge. To shine in the court and to express his courtesy towards women, a man needed wide reading and some skill with the pen: 'Let him', the authority continued, 'much exercise himself in poets,

Education of a prince: Maximilian Sforza at his lessons. From Donatus, *Grammatica*, 15th Cent.

and no less in orators and historiographers, and also in writing both rime and prose, and specially in this our vulgar tongue. For beside the contentation that he shall receive thereby himself, he shall by this means never want pleasant entertainments with women which ordinarily love such matters.'

If that encouragement to learning went a little beyond former chivalry, the rest of the message was thoroughly orthodox. Pride, Chastellain had written, was the sharpest spur to noble natures, and Castiglione agreed that in all great matters 'the true provocation is glory'. Learning was one way to win glory; other ways were to have a graceful and elegant presence (but not effeminate), to ride perfectly, to handle easily all kinds of weapons, to hunt and hawk, to swim, leap, run, vault and play at tennis (but not to tumble, walk the tightrope, or juggle, which were all unfit for gentlemen), to be a musician skilful on several instruments, and generally to frame oneself to company, having all the arts of agreeable intercourse: 'let him laugh, dally, jest, and dance, yet in such wise that he may always declare himself to be witty and discreet, and everything that he doeth or speaketh, let him do it with a grace'. The discipline required was difficult to learn and arduous to practise, but the attempt was worth while, for only by demonstrating these qualities could a man achieve the 'flower of courtliness', and reap the honours and rewards due to this high estate.

The training designed to civilize feudal cavalry sufficed, with very little change, to breed the aristocratic refinement of the Renaissance courtier. And the gentleman of today is still a man from the same mould, wearing his knowledge lightly, neither pedantic nor profound, a dilettante of the arts, thoroughly sporting, fit, healthy and active, but above all affable, elegant, courteous and correct. Good manners, as the west understands them, are but the gloss of latter ages on the doctrine of medieval chivalry. To give way to a lady, even to lay the knife on the right of the plate, is to salute at a great distance certain courtly innovators in twelfth-century Languedoc, and to acknowledge, however faintly, the force of a poetic ideal.

Renaissance courtesy belonged to aristocrats. As chivalry became the property of a class, so chivalric and courtly virtues were generally considered exclusive aristocratic virtues. 'I will have this our courtier,' said Castiglione, 'therefore, to be a gentleman born and of a good house.' The reason given was the familiar argument, heard so often in the court of Burgundy, that only pride of birth could drive men to noble action: 'For nobleness of birth is (as it were) a clear lamp that sheweth forth and bringeth into light, works both good and bad, and enflameth and provoketh unto virtue, as well with fear of slander, as also with the hope of praise.' Besides, the world was class-ridden (Castiglione went on) whether we liked it or not, and the qualities of a gentleman were not only those expected by the high born of themselves, but also those expected of them by the lower orders whom a nobleman should not disappoint. 'For where there are two in a nobleman's house which at the first have given no proof of themselves with good works or bad, as soon as it is known

Romantic conventions: nostalgia for
the simple, pastoral life; the game of
'la maine chaude' played amid the
flocks. Tournai School, 16th Cent.

that one is a gentleman born, and the other not, the unnoble shall be much less esteemed with every man, than the gentleman.'

But there were still some who understood chivalry in the original sense, not as manners but as morality, not the property of a class but the virtue of a people. Pride in ancient riches (as Chaucer put it) is presumptuous gentility—'such arrogance is not worth a hen':

> Look who that is most virtuous alway,
> Privy and apart, and most entendeth ay
> To do the gentle deeds that he can,
> And take him for the greatest gentle man.
> Christ wills, we claim of him our gentleness,
> Not of our elders for their old richness.

Idealists undeceived by the noble's presumptuous claim saw courtesy not as the glint on an aristocrat but as the ethical mark of a people, and they still looked on chivalry, rightly applied according to the 'goodly usage of those antique times, in which the sword was servant unto right', to make order shine in the night of chaos. The world succeeding on feudalism was still painfully wrong, as it remains to this day. But was not the ideal of chivalry devised for just such a world, to fight 'gainst tortuous power and lawless regiment'? If chivalry was a generous force, capable of making moral order out of political chaos, who could be better than the poet to propound the law of courtesy? For was not the ideal in part the creation of poets, of troubadours and trouvères?

Poetry was still equal to this high office, to assert the ideal of chivalric order against the ravage of time and polity. It was Orpheus, said one writer, 'who by the sweet gift of his heavenly poetry withdrew men from ranging uncertainty and wandering brutishly about, and made them gather together and keep company, make houses and keep fellowship together'; it was Orpheus, said another, who 'by his discreet and wholesome lessons uttered in harmony and with melodious instruments brought rude and savage people to a more civil and orderly life'. In the last completed book of *The Faerie Queen*, Edmund Spenser attempted the work of Orpheus and did what the troubadours had done before; he set down for all troubled times the vision of a pastoral world ruled by chivalric courtesy. In the allegory of the Sixth Book, the perfect chevalier Sir Calidore adventures into pastures of simple delight and honest emotion, 'the sacred nursery of virtue', and finds in this peaceful seclusion:

>              not a fairer flower,
> Than is the blossom of comely courtesy,
> Which though it on a lowly stalk do bower,
> Yet brancheth forth in brave nobility,
> And spreads itself through all civility.

The land of uncorrupted shepherds is the only place left free by the Blatant Beast of disorder, and inspired by the harmony of lives brought up in natural courtesy Sir Calidore redoubles his search for the Beast who has ravaged with 'many massacres' all the other estates of the world, to bind down the monster of chaos with bonds of courtesy.

But the poet sadly knew that his allegory was not the true picture of the world. The polity of art was not yet realized. The Blatant Beast, that 'rends without regard of person or of time', was loose once more:

> So now he rangeth through the world again,
> And rageth sore in each degree and state;
> Nor any is, that may him now restrain,
> He growen is so great and strong of late.

Dreams of the ideal awaken to reality. But amid ignoble actions and the squalor made by man and money, the land of courtesy so temptingly conceived by the poets of chivalry still promises release to weary spirits.

Poets despaired of a world run wrong, of their ideal spurned and themselves neglected. 'Where have all the jongleurs fled,' Giraut de Borneil wondered, 'who were once so well received?' Despondent Riquier, the last of his troubadour kind, agreed that 'no calling is now less appreciated in noble courts than the fine art of poetry'. In the stricken land of Languedoc, ripped up by the Albigensian Crusade, the poet ceased to be the henchman of princes and the celebrated arbiter of life. But the lyrical mode that the troubadour had dis-

The diffusion of the Arthurian legend: the abduction of Guinevere, a relief from Modena Cathedral, *c.* 1100.

covered, and the romantic matter that the trouvère had added to it, did not die away. In bad times, what else was there for the poet to do but sing his characteristic song? And the times that hurt the poet helped his poetry, for the joy and love and stirring deeds of the new verse comforted the oppressed. Art succeeds very often when policy fails. Common stories gave common ground for all European peoples. The literary manner that sprang up so strangely in twelfth-century Languedoc became the taste of Europe, reconciling, in imagination at least, the people of Norway and Sweden with those of Italy and Spain.

And in the mass of fiction that gave a common delight, no stories were more famous than the amorous and gallant deeds of the court of King Arthur of Britain. Where these stories were born and how they grew is still obscure. Most likely they were of Celtic origin and were spread about by the Normans, those foot-loose warriors, whose wandering conquests planted them on the borders of Celtic Wales and Brittany, from where they took the Arthurian lore to France, and then onward even to Greece and the frontier of the Moslem world. This was the new fashion, the 'matter of Britain' displacing the 'matter of France', the older epic of Charlemagne and Roland. The old *chansons de geste* were the poetry of action, the deeds of mighty warriors, the new lore was the poetry of sentiment, the love and gallantry of courtiers. The subtle art of Chrétien de Troyes finally established the tone and conventions of this romance, and the poets of France and Germany, followed later by those of the rest of Europe, ardently propagated this amorous, courteous faith. The court of Arthur became the model of chivalrous enterprise through-out the west. 'Behold that noble king of Britain, King Arthur,' Caxton exhorted his countrymen in the degenerate days of the late fifteenth century, 'with all the noble knights of the Round Table whose noble acts and noble chivalry of his knights occupy so many large volumes. O ye knights of England where is the custom and usage of noble chivalry that was used in those days? What do ye now but go to the baths and play at dice? And some not well advised, use not honest and good rule, against all order of knighthood. Leave this, leave it, and read the noble volumes of Saint Graal, of Lancelot, of Galahad, of Tristram, of Perceforest, of Perceval, of Gawain, and many more. There shall ye see manhood, courtesy and gentleness.'

Possessed by the spirit of the Arthurian adventure, tutored in 'courtesy and gentleness', the poet became the 'clerk of love'; as Geoffrey Chaucer said of himself, and his words typically applied to so many others, he had 'told of lovers up and down more than Ovid maketh of mention'. Love, as Dante's Francesca says, was the necessity of every gentle heart. The celebration of love was the first gift that the troubadours had given to chivalry, and chivalry ever after demanded the proper service of the mischievous deity. Castiglione, teaching his courtier 'how to love contrary to the wonted manner of the common ignorant sort', prayed that 'it may be granted the courtier, while he is young, to love sensually'. And then in courtly wisdom he had a duty to give his lady romantic service: 'Afterward let him obey, please, and honour with all reverence his woman, and reckon her more dear to him than his own life, and prefer all her commodities and pleasures before his own, and love no less in her the beauty of the mind, than of the body.'

How far the doctrine was followed in practice is impossible to say. At any rate, it was the ideal of the gentleman, delightful to read, offering escape for a little while from rough reality to gentler worlds, enabling a man to become completely in imagination, if not in act, a romantic lover. The chivalrous gentleman, says the knowing lady to her young servitor in *Le Petit Jehan de Saintré*, is nothing if he is not a lover. 'This true and faithful lover,' she instructs him, 'that is of gentle birth, whole and sound in mind and body, pursueth day and night his amorous quest for the favour of his fair lady, the which gentle lady shall be above all others (I call them ladies all, for in love all are ladies).' And since the lad John was well into his teens, it was time he forgot his bashfulness and followed love seriously. 'You love none?' cried the lady. 'O recreant knight, do you say that you love none? By this I know well that you shall never be a man of worship. Why, faint-heart, from where came the high prowess, the mighty enterprises and knightly deeds of Lancelot, of Gawain, of Tristram, of Giron the courteous, and the other warriors of the Round Table, and so many other valiant knights and squires of this kingdom and others beyond number (that I could well rehearse had I time), if it were not from seeking to serve love and to uphold them in the favour of their most beloved ladies?' Was Little John not handsome, noble, vigorous and eager? his temptress continued. Why was he so backward when her own heart could be his reward? And with many modest blushes Little John of Saintré came to chivalrous manhood.

That was the pattern for gentle conduct. From the first moment that he could lay claim to any sort of wit (the Black Knight confessed in Chaucer's *Book of the Duchess*), he was wound up for love, a servant already in anticipation, body, heart and all, before ever he had an object for his devotion. He was like a blank page or canvas, awaiting the tender imprint of the beloved; and the minute he saw her 'dance so comely, carol and sing so sweetly, laugh and play so womanly, and look so debonairly' the tight spring of his heart was tripped, and she became at once:

> My suffisaunce, my lust, my life,
> Mine hap, mine heal, and all my bliss,
> My worldes welfare and my liss,
> And I hers wholly, everydel.

The influence of the poets had elaborated within chivalry two kinds of courtesy, and nothing portrayed both so clearly or so affectionately as the Prologue to Chaucer's *Canterbury Tales*. First, there was the ideal worthiness of the Knight, who so 'loved chivalry, truth and honour, freedom and courtesy' that he had spent his life on the wars of Christendom following the old teaching of military chivalry, a faithful Christian *prudhomme*, brave, modest and pious, soberly dressed in worn fustian rubbed threadbare by armour. This was the man that Chaucer loved best, the one whose quiet authority governed so easily the riotous outbursts of anger and vainglory, of

Knights departing in search of the Holy Grail.

vulgarity and licentiousness which punctuated that eventful pilgrimage to the tomb of St Thomas à Becket. And then there was the Knight's son, the Squire, the young embodiment of all elegance and all courtliness. Here was the chevalier lover in all his glory, with hair curled as if from a press, and his person embroidered like a meadow 'all full of fresh flowers, white and red'. Young as he was, he had already been to the wars as became a knight, though his campaigns had taken him only to the near fields of Flanders, Artois and Picardy, and his warlike gallantry was planned (unlike the severe prowess of his father) to help him 'stonden in his lady's grace'. Singing and fluting were as much his passion as riding and arms:

> He could songes make and well endite,
> Joust and eek dance, and well portray and write.
> So hot he loved, that by night at all
> He slept no more than does a nightingale.

The full-dressed romantic gallant had arrived. And just how well he possessed the imagination may be judged by the protests of sober moralists against his universal presence and popularity in the literature. The whole pleasure of Malory's *Morte d'Arthur*, complained the censorious Elizabethan school master Roger Ascham, 'standeth in open manslaughter and bold bawdry—in which book those be counted the noblest knights that do kill most men without any quarrel, and commit the foulest adulteries by subtlest shifts'.

For the doctrine that the poet gave to the new gentleman was the old religion of love, imperious and adulterous, founded by the troubadours and developed by the court-writers of the noble ladies who ruled in Aquitaine and Champagne. Bondage and sensuality, which the *Roman de la Rose* had so strongly yoked, were the true marks of romance. Love was a capricious god:

> Love will not be constrained by mastery;
> When mastery cometh, the god of love anon
> Beateth his wings, and farewell! he is gone!
> Love is a thing as any spirit free.

Where his darts might fall none could tell, but they were so potent they compelled obedience. The tyranny of love, which overrode both decency and compassion, was brought home by the cruel little story of the *Chevalier au Chainse*—'the Knight of the Bloody Shirt'. In this Gothic tale, a lady sent a shirt to each of three knights who vied for her love, declaring that she would accept the one who fought in a tourney with no protection other than the light shirt. Two refused. The third accepted, was woefully hacked about, and then returned the pierced and bloody shirt to the lady, begging her to wear it for his sake, flaunting it at the feast before her husband and all the nobles. 'I will gladly,' said the lady. 'Since it was wet with the blood of my loyal servant, I hold it a dress fit for a queen. For no jewel could be more precious to me than the blood that stains it.' The prize of love is worth the risk of the life of one, and the reputation of the other.

Love required suffering and trial which, successfully overcome, won undying merit that was, in its way, akin to salvation. In the *Morte d'Arthur*, Elaine told her confessor that her love for Lancelot was excused, for 'I loved never none but him, nor never shall, of earthly creature'; in the midst of her love she was, in her own view, a 'clean maiden', and she thought the torments she had suffered for love were penance enough for any sin she might have committed. On the matter of love the poets were inconsistent and contradictory. One liked to dwell on the cruelty of love, another emphasized the passion, a third the fidelity, a fourth the pathos. But all generally hold that it is an irresistible onslaught that needs no excuse and accepts no reward other than the mutual satisfaction of the lovers. Love, says Dante's Francesca, is that which begets love. It is the service of the one by the other; the man is servant, not husband, to the lady, and he to her is lord, not spouse.

The way of faith, which the Church sternly maintained, was hard, unremitting, unkindly contemptuous of natural desires. There was, in the poets of chivalry, a compensating religion, a purely human faith of kindliness and satisfaction, acknowledging (as the Church would not do) the force of passion. 'Well I wot that love is a great mistress,' says Lancelot in the *Morte d'Arthur*. Neither is it an unworthy mistress, for it is love, Malory adds, that makes the springtime in the human heart: 'Therefore, like as May month flowers and flourishes in every man's garden, so in like wise let every man of

*Above.* A scene from the Court of Burgundy.

*Left.* Geoffrey Chaucer, court poet and the 'clerk of love', presents his works at the court of Richard II. From a 15th Cent manuscript.

worship flourish his heart in this world, first unto God and next unto the joy of them that he promised his faith unto. For there was never worshipful man nor worshipful woman but they loved one better than another, and worship in arms may never be foiled.' Only abandonment to this 'worshipful way' can lead to the bliss which the minnesinger Gottfried von Strassburg reserved for the Tristan and Isolde of his poem: 'Their high feast was love, who gilded all their joys. Love brought them as homage the Round Table and all its company a thousand times a day. What better food could they have for body or soul? Man was there with woman, and woman there with man. What else should they be needing? They had what they were meant to have. They had reached the goal of their desire.'

The authors were aware, and none more so than Malory, that the amorous doctrine of chivalry was against the teaching of the Church. 'But first reserve the honour of God,' Malory cautioned, 'and secondly thy quarrel must come of thy lady. And such love I call virtuous

237

love.' Virtuous love shunned flightiness or mere sexual gratification: 'this is no wisdom neither no stability but it is feebleness of nature and great disworship'. Inconstancy, said Malory, was the modern manner, which had fallen away from the true ideal. 'But nowadays men cannot love seven-nights but they must have all their desires. That love may not endure by reason, for where they are soon accorded and hasty, heat soon cools. And right so fares the love nowadays, soon hot, soon cold. This is no stability. But the old love was not so, for men and women could love together seven years and no licorous lusts was between them, and then was love, truth and faithfulness. And so in like wise was used such love in King Arthur's days.' Romantic love, served with constancy, seemed a kind of natural sacrament which, since it had the assent of the heart, could not be wrong, though an ungracious Church might find it a technical sin. 'God', wrote Andreas Capellanus, the scholiast of love, 'cannot be seriously offended by love, for what is done under the compulsion of nature can be made clean by an easy expiation.' That, too, was the opinion of Malory, a plain soldier without the subtleties of argument but with a knowledge of the human heart. 'Why should I leave such thoughts?' says Elaine to her confessor who condemns her infatuation. 'Am I not an earthly woman? And all the while the breath is in my body I may complain

*Above.* Lancelot and Queen Guinevere. From the *Lancelot du Lac*, 13th Cent.

*Left.* Romantic love: the offering of the heart in the rose garden; the lady has her falcon on her fist. 15th Cent.

me, for my belief is that I do none offence, though I love an earthly man, unto God, for He formed me thereto.'

But to moralists such as Ascham this reasonable theory was little more than dishonest pleading. The stories of chivalry made it quite clear that romantic passion was naturally illicit, and very often tragic. Among the great number of goodly knights and noble ladies in the *Morte d'Arthur* there is but one example of married love. Lancelot may easily reject casual offers of love, and even marriage, partly on the old military ground that to accept he would have to leave 'armies and tournaments, battles and adventures', and partly because an acceptance would indicate nothing but common lechery. But the fatal attraction of Guinevere, Arthur's Queen, could not be resisted, and the true knight, as Sir Bors advised Lancelot, would not hesitate to serve her, for love now bound them despite all morality. 'And also

241

I will council you, my lord,' said Bors, 'that my lady, Queen Guinevere, and she be in any distress, insomuch as she is in pain for your sake, that you knightly rescue her; for, and you did any other wise, all the world would speak you shame to the world's end. Insomuch as you were taken with her, whether you did right or wrong, it is now your part to hold with the Queen.'

There could be no better indication of a world well lost for love, and Malory, whatever he might have intended in support of morality, makes Lancelot and the Queen in their conduct confirm this. Lancelot, the perfect knight, lies and cheats for the sake of Guinevere, destroys the court of the Round Table with the passion of his illicit love, and brings about the death of his noble lord King Arthur. 'Through this same man and me', admits the repentant Queen, 'has all this war been wrought and the death of the most noblest knights of the world. For through our love that we have loved together is my most noble lord slain. And therefore, Sir Lancelot, I require thee and beseech thee heartily, for all the love that ever was betwixt us, that thou never see me no more in the visage.' And Lancelot, if he must reluctantly obey, begs one more unrepentant kiss, 'for I take record of God, in you I have had my earthly joy'.

Not even Arthur condemned the lovers who caused his death, and what heart from that day to this has blamed them? The powers of chivalrous imagination have bewitched all ages. That love should be true is its only necessity, that it may be tragic only makes it more poignant. When the Reformation broke the fetters of the Church, and the restraint of religion relaxed year by year, then the romantic faith of the writers of love won myriads of converts to the belief in the heart, for every man and woman could perceive the strength of the chivalric promise, that the arrival of love heralded the spring of life; 'for then all herbs and trees renew a man and woman, and in like wise lovers call to their mind old gentleness and old service and many kind deeds that was forgotten by negligence'. Spring, we know, gives way to winter; experience soon sobers intoxicated youth; 'fair Criseyde', the timid girl who loved her Troilus all to well, became in time 'false Criseyde', the helpless woman made faithless by adversity.

But in the time of their loving what joy, what fulfilment, Troilus and Criseyde had of each other. In Chaucer's radiant poem, the Provençal dawn of light and love matured into full day. The homage to the deity sang along the sinews of the heart. The 'blissful light', daughter of Jove, penetrated heaven and hell, the earth, the salt sea; man, all beasts, all growing things feel its effective power:

God loveth, and to love will nought deny;
And in this world no living creature,
With-outen love, is worth, or may endure.

In May, 'the mother of glad months', who could be so arrogant, so blind as to avoid love? Troilus, a king's son and the pride of Troy, happy as Bayard in the strength of his arm, 'yet with a look his heart waxed a-fear, that he, that now was most in pride above, waxed suddenly most subject unto love'. You wise, proud and worthy people, says the poet, it is pointless to resist:

> For ever it was, and ever it shall befall,
> That Love is he that all things may bind;
> For may no man for-do the law of kind.

Troilus the warrior is reborn into grace and courtesy. Tender, fearful Criseyde blooms into the rose of the world, perceiving through her beloved a new order in existence; for she tells him that it was not his royal birth, nor his worthiness, nor prowess, riches, looks, nor even 'vain delight' that won her to him, 'but moral virtue, grounded upon truth'. This perhaps was not the morality the Church spoke of, but the natural order of the free expression of the free heart. Both know how greatly they are uplifted and made whole by the influence of love:

> Benign love, thou holy bond of things,
> Whoso will grace, and list thee nought honours,
> Lo, his desire will flee with-outen wings,

In the luminous glow of the 'bent moon with the pale horns' the lovers met and timorously touched, not celebrating the marriage contract, but the more sovereign rites of love, she shaking like an aspen-leaf and he with the resolution of the warrior:

> Pleasure of love, O goodly debonaire
> In gentle hearts all ready to repair!
> O very cause of heal and of gladness,
> All blessed be thy might and thy goodness!

Afterwards came the pain, the clash of war, the lovers torn apart by political expediency, poor Criseyde driven to betray her love, and Troilus killed:

> Such is this world, whoso it can behold:
> In each estate is little heartes rest.
> God leave us for to take it for the best!

What happened was the ordinary expectation of an earthly love that guaranteed no safety from the hurts of time, and which Chaucer, the Christian poet, saw transcended by the holy force of heavenly love.

Love is a constant theme of all history, but nowhere was it sanctified and praised as it was in chivalry, which made of it an extraordinary pageant, a triumph in death as in life. Chivalrous Chaucer found nature fulfilled through the operation of love; only through it did men and women become most fair, most gentle, most kind, most generous. For chivalrous Spenser, love was a sacred fire that purged 'base affections and filthy lust from brutish minds', a pure fire that lit the lamp of beauty and kindled 'all noble deeds and never dying flame'. Dante, in whose powerful mind the holy and the profane opposites of chivalry were reconciled, knew that 'love drew his thought from all vile things', and out of the stammering passion he felt for Beatrice in the streets of Florence he made the august Love

that moves the universe; at the summit of the mount of Purgatory, Beatrice appears to take him by the hand and lead him to the sublime heights to which Virgil, the man of reason, cannot take him.

Those who worship love create for themselves a fallible god, and there was a side of chivalry that knew and expressed this only too well. In several of the troubadours, in the final part of the *Roman de la Rose*, in Deschamps and Villon, in such works as the *XV Joys of Marriage*, there was very often a rancorous or cynical misogyny that sneered at the elevation of women. Nor did the practice of the world follow the spirit of the ideal. Women were still traded for the convenience of policy or inheritance; the dull prison of marriage was infinitely more likely than the boudoir of romantic passion. Women, as the knight of La Tour Landry warned his daughters, were considered subservient beings and must beware the strong arm of their husbands.

But the mythology of romance founded on chivalry has endured against all criticism and all practice. Guinevere and Lancelot, Tristan and Isolde are still the exemplars for western ages. The melodious triumphs, the sighs and deaths of lovers taken beyond reason by tyrannous passion are the images in the most persistent dream of our society. The tawdry art of women's magazine and popular song acknowledge a world well lost for love. What are these but the corruption and degeneration of a great tradition, crude reflections of unforgettable moments, of Juliet fearing the lark that summons Romeo away, of Cleopatra applying the asp to her imperial breast, of a hundred thousand lovers who knew suffering and consummation and, like the swan, sang before dying?

Evidence of romantic feeling: a 15th Cent effigy in romantic pose, in contrast to the austerity of earlier sepulchral figures. The Greene Monument, Lowick.

# acknowledgements

CHAPTER 1
pp. 7: Bern Historische museum; 8: Stockholm, Historical museum/M. Dixon; 10: Aachen, basilica/Scala; 11a: Amiens, bibliothèque/F. Garnier; 11b: St Gall psalter/G. Goldner; 12: Stockholm Historical museum; 13: Stockholm Historical museum/M. Holford; 14: New York, Pierpont Morgan library, MS. 736, fol. 12v; 17: Heidelberg bibliothek/Snark; 20: Arras bibliothèque, MS. 559/F. Garnier; 22: Dijon bibliothèque/F. Garnier; 23: Bern, Burgerbibliothek; 24: Clermont-Ferrand/Janet le Caisne; 25: M. Dixon; 26: Bern, Burgerbibliothek.

CHAPTER 2
pp. 28: Lanaud; 29: London, British Library, MS. 20 C VII, fol. 136b; 30: Janet le Caisne; 31: Le Mans, bibliothèque, MS. 228/F. Garnier; 33a: Madrid, Biblioteca nacional, Codex Skyllitzes, fol. 730v/Oronoz; 33b: same, fol. 108v; 34: Paris, Bibliothèque Nationale/Snark; 35: Meaux, musée municipal/A. Held; 36a: Barcelona, museum of Catalan art/A. Held; 36b: Paris, Bibliothèque Nationale/G. Goldner; 37: Santiago de Compostella, Codex Calixtinus, fol. 162v/Oronoz; 38: Janet le Caisne; 39: Paris, Bibliothèque de l'Arsenal, MS. 3142, fol. 129/Giraudon; 40a: Barcelona, museum of Catalan art/A. Held; 40b: Monte Cassino, M. Rabano: De Bellis, p. 474/Scala; 41: Pernes (Vaucluse)/A. Held; 42: Paris, Bibliothèque Nationale, MS. fr. 99, fol. 561; 44: Paris, Bibliothèque Nationale, MS. lat. 12302, fol. 1; 45: Paris, Bibliothèque Nationale, MS. lat. 8846, fol. 156v/G. Goldner; 47: Chartres museum/M. Slingsby; 48: Chartres cathedral/M. Babey; 49: Paris, Bibliothèque Ste Geneviève, MS. 394/F. Garnier; 50: Archives Nationales/Janet le Caisne; 51: F. Garnier; 52: Paris, Bibliothèque Nationale, MS. fr. 2628, fol. 145; 53: Janet le Caisne.

CHAPTER 3
pp. 55: Oxford, Bodleian library, MS. Bodley 264; 56: same; 57: Bourges, préfecture/Janet le Caisne; 58: same as 55; 59: Chantilly, musée Condé, MS. 433/590, fol. 45v/Giraudon; 60: Paris, Bibliothèque Nationale/G. Goldner; 61: Oxford, Bodleian library, MS. Tanner 190; 62: Paris, Bibliothèque Nationale, MS. lat. 1118, fol. 112v; 64/65: Florence, palazzo Davanzati/Scala; 69: Paris, Bibliothèque Nationale, MS. fr. 2630, fol. 63v; 70a: Paris, Bibliothèque Nationale, MS. fr. 773, fol. 51v; 70b: Madrid, Escorial/Oronoz; 71: Ribière; 72: Ribière; 73: Paris, Bibliothèque Nationale, MS. lat. 886, fol. 4v; 74: London, British Library, Add. MS. 42130; 75: Cambridge, Pembroke College, MS. 120, fol. 2v; 76: New York, Pierpont Morgan library, MS. 917, fol. 180;

78: Paris, Bibliothèque Nationale, MS. fr. 12400, fol. 135; 79: M. Holford; 81a: Siena, palazzo publico/Scala; 81b: Florence, palazzo Davanzati/Scala.

CHAPTER 4
pp. 82a: Paris, Bibliothèque Nationale, MS. fr. 1586, fol. 56; 82b: Chantilly, musée Condé, MS. 137/F. Garnier; 83: Chantilly, musée Condé/F. Garnier; 84: Oronoz; 85: Oronoz; 85k: Heidelberg University library/Hansmann; 86: Paris, Bibliothèque Nationale, MS. fr. 836, fol. 65; 88: Scala; 89a: Paris, Bibliothèque Ste Geneviève, MS. 1371–9–, fol. 125v/F. Garnier; 89b: same, MS. 1126; 90: Brussels, Bibliothèque Royale Albert 1, MS. 9466, fol. 4rD, cat. 129; 92: Scala; 93: Paris, Bibliothèque Ste Geneviève, MS. 246/F. Garnier; 94: Oxford, Bodleian library, MS. Douce 332, fol. 153v; 95: Carpentras, Bibliothèque Inguimbertine, MS. 403, fol. 7v; 96: F. Garnier; 98: Chantilly, musée Condé, MS. XIV H 27–482 (665), fol. 108r/Laffont; 99: Paris, Bibliothèque Nationale, MS. fr. 854, fol. 123r/Laffont; 100: Madrid, Escorial – London, Victoria & Albert museum; 101: Paris, Bibliothèque Nationale; 102: Montpellier University, MS. 196/J. Hyde; 103: Cleveland museum of art, MS. 53152; 106: Janet le Caisne; 108: London, British Library, Add. MS. 42130, fol. 181v–182r; 109: Paris, musée de Cluny/F. Garnier; 111: Ribière; 113: Ribière.

CHAPTER 5
pp. 115: Janet le Caisne; 116: Autun cathedral/Janet le Caisne; 119: London, British Library, MS. Royal 14 C VII, fol. 2–4; 120: London, British Library, MS. Royal 14 C VII, fol. 3–4; 121: Paris, Bibliothèque Nationale/Snark; 122: R. Sheridan; 124a: R. Sheridan; 124b: Oxford, Bodleian library, MS. Laud misc. 587, fol. 1; 125: R. Sheridan; 126: London, British Library, MS. Nero E II, vol. 1/Laffont; 127a: Oxford, Bodleian library, MS. Tanner 190; 127b: Paris, Bibliothèque Nationale, MS. fr. 13568, fol. 83; 129: R. Sheridan; 130: Paris, Bibliothèque Nationale, Fonds arabe 5847, fol. 94; 132a: Paris, Bibliothèque Nationale/G. Goldner; 132b: Madrid, Biblioteca Nacional, MS. 195/Oronoz; 133a: M. Holford; 133b: Baltimore, Walters art gallery; 134: Oxford, Bodleian library, MS. Tanner 190, 204v–205; 135: Lyon, bibliothèque, MS. 828, fol. 83r/F. Garnier; 136: Baltimore, Walters art gallery; 137: Oxford, Bodleian library, MS. Bodley 968; 138: F. Garnier; 139: R. Sheridan; 140: Paris, Bibliothèque de l'Arsenal, 'Gouvernement des princes', fol. 149v/G. Goldner; 141: St Floret castle, Templars chapel/A. Held; 142: Paris, Bibliothèque Ste Geneviève, MS. 782/F. Garnier; 144a: Editions Théojac; 144b: Toulouse,

Editions Larrey; 145: Lyon, bibliothèque, MS. 828, fol. 205v/F. Garnier; 146: Paris, Bibliothèque Nationale, MS. fr. 22495, fol. 215v/Snark; 147: Janet le Caisne; 151: R. Sheridan.

## CHAPTER 6

pp. 153: Paris, Bibliothèque Ste Geneviève/F. Garnier; 154: Ribière; 156: Paris, Louvre museum/Archives photo; 157: Paris, Bibliothèque Ste Geneviève, MS. 329/ F. Garnier; 158: London, British Library, MS. Sloane 2435, fol. 44r; 159: Paris, Archives Nationales/Giraudon; 160: London, British Museum/Hansmann; 161: Snark; 162: Ribière; 164: Snark; 165: Paris, Bibliothèque Ste Geneviève, MS. 331/F. Garnier; 166: Ribière; 167: Marseille, Archives des Bouches du Rhône; 168: Paris, Bibliothèque Nationale; 170: M. Dixon; 171: F. Garnier; 172: Paris, Bibliothèque Nationale, MS. fr. 2644/Snark; 176: Paris, Bibliothèque Nationale/G. Goldner; 178: Paris, Bibliothèque Nationale/Snark; 179: same.

## CHAPTER 7

pp. 182: Brussels, Bibliothèque Royale Albert 1, MS. 130-71-76, fol. 24v; 184: Lübeck, Ste Anne museum; 185: Paris, Louvre museum/Giraudon; 186: London, British Library, MS. 36619, f⁶l. 5-545r; 188: London, British Library, MS. Harley 6199, fol. 57v; 189: Paris, Bibliothèque Nationale, MS. lat. 9471, fol. 7r; 190/191: Versailles castle/Giraudon; 193: Paris, Bibliothèque Ste Geneviève, MS. 814/F. Garnier; 196: Nantes, musée Dobrée, MS. Antoine Dufour, fol. 76/Giraudon; 198/199: Paris, Bibliothèque de l'Arsenal, MS. fr. 2695, fol. 67-68; 200: London, Victoria & Albert museum/ M. Holford; 201: Baltimore, Walters art gallery, MS. 10.313, fol 10v; 202: London, British Library, Cotton MS. Julius E IV, fol. 203; 203: Paris, Bibliothèque Nationale, MS. fr. 2695, fol. 100v-101; 204: Oxford, Bodleian library, MS. Douce 383; 206: Oxford, Bodleian library, MS. Douce 374, fol. 17; 209a: Paris, Bibliothèque Nationale/G. Goldner; 209b: Paris, Petit Palais, HV 330, fol. 110/Laffont; 210: Chantilly, musée Condé, MS. 834-314/ Giraudon; 211: Oxford, Bodleian library, MS. Rawl. D 1220, fol. 31v; 212: Dijon museum/ G. Goldner; 213a: Paris, Bibliothèque Ste Geneviève/ F. Garnier; 213b: Hansmann; 214: Paris, musée de Cluny/M. Slingsby; 215: Oxford, Bodleian library, MS. Douce 195, fol. 7; 216: Paris, Bibliothèque Nationale, MS. lat. 17294, fol. 448; 217a: Madrid, Prado/Scala; 217b: Paris, musée de Cluny/ R. Roland.

## CHAPTER 8

pp. 219a: Paris, Bibliothèque Nationale, MS. fr. 95, fol. 326; 219b: same, MS. fr. 2092, fol. 10v; 220: New York, Pierpont Morgan library, MS. 917; 221: National Trust; 222: Paris, Bibliothèque de l'Arsenal, MS. fr. 5073/Giraudon; 223: Paris, Bibliothèque Nationale; 224a: Gotha, Schloss museum/Hansmann; 224b: Vienna, National Library, MS. 2597, fol. 15r/A. Held; 225: Munich, Bayer. Staatsgemäldesammlungen; 227: Milan, Trevulziana library, MS. 2167, fol. 13v; 229: R. Sheridan; 234: Paris, Bibliothèque Nationale, MS. fr. 343, fol. 8v; 236: Cambridge, Corpus Christi College, MS. 61, fol. IV; 237: Paris, Bibliothèque de l'Arsenal, MS. 5087, fol. 144v/J. Hyde; 238: Chantilly, musée Condé/Giraudon; 239: Munich, Bayer. National museum/Hansmann; 240: Paris, musée de Cluny/ R. Roland; 241: Paris, Bibliothèque Nationale, MS. fr. 119, fol. CCXXXI/Laffont; 244: R. Sheridan.

Photographic material from MM. Held, Roland, Garnier, Babey, and Oronoz has been obtained through Mr Joseph Ziolo.

# index

pages 87-96 missing

| DATE DUE | | | |
|----------|---|---|---|
| FEB 2 '80 | | | |
| APR 8 '81 | | | |
| MAR 23 '85 | | | |
| | | | |
| | | | |
| | | | |
| | | | |
| | | | |
| | | | |
| | | | |
| | | | |
| | | | |
| | | | |